D0122156

HENRY WADSWORTH
LONGFELLOW

Selected
Poems

HENRY WADSWORTH LONGFELLOW

Selected Poems

GRAMERCY BOOKS
New York

Introduction
Copyright © 1992 by Random House Value Publishing, Inc.
All rights reserved

This 1992 edition is published by Gramercy Books,
distributed by Random House Value Publishing, Inc.,
201 East 50th Street, New York, New York 10022,

Random House
New York • Toronto • London • Sydney • Auckland

http://www.randomhouse.com/

Printed and bound in the United States

Library of Congress Cataloging-in-Publication Data
Longfellow, Henry Wadsworth, 1807-1882.
[Poems. Selections]
Selected poems of Henry Wadsworth Longfellow.
p. cm.
ISBN 0-517-08246-2
I. Title
PS2253 1992
811'.3—dc20   92-12783   CIP

CONTENTS

Introduction   7

Shorter Lyric and Narrative Poems

Evangeline, A Tale of Acadie

From The Song of Hiawatha

The Courtship of Miles Standish

INTRODUCTION

When Henry Wadsworth Longfellow died on March 24, 1882, he was the most popular poet in the English-speaking world. Not only was he America's first professional poet, but, after his death, he was the first American whose bust was placed in the Poet's Corner at Westminster Abbey in London, England.

Longfellow was born on February 27, 1807 in Portland, Maine. He came from a long, distinguished line of upperclass New Englanders. His father was a lawyer, a judge, and a member of Congress. When the young Longfellow enrolled at Bowdoin College, it was expected that he would follow in his father's footsteps. But he was adverse to the prospect of a career in law and wrote to his father, "I utterly and absolutely detest it." He wanted to write but he knew his father would not consider it a suitable profession. A compromise was eventually reached; Longfellow would become the professor of modern languages at Bowdoin, a position established expressly for him (his father was a trustee of the college). After he was graduated in 1826, he spent three years in France, Spain, Italy, and Germany preparing himself for his new post. And, indeed, he became fluent in all four languages and able to competently read Swedish, Finnish, Danish, Norwegian, Dutch, and Portuguese.

Although Longfellow felt teaching interfered with his writing, he nonetheless became a distinguished professor at Bowdoin, where he taught from 1829 until 1835, and then at Harvard as the Smith Professor of Modern Languages, a position he gave up in 1854 after he began to earn enough money from his poetry. Longfellow was one of the great educators of the American public. He had an extensive knowledge of European literature and became one of its principal disseminators through his many translations, which included Dante's *Divine Comedy*. This knowledge was the foundation for his own poetry as a great part of his poetic genius lay in his ability to experiment with and adapt preexisting verse forms to a distinctly American context and subject matter. This can clearly be seen in *The Song of Hiawatha*, his retelling of the story of a legendary Onondaga Indian chieftain, in which the eight-syllable trochaic line used throughout was borrowed from *Kalevala*, the Finnish national epic, or in *Evangeline*, his pastoral tale of star-crossed lovers in Nova Scotia, in which he used the hexameter line from Classical Greek poetry.

Longfellow was an unsurpassed master of musical language. Only Tennyson and Edgar Allan Poe at their best could match his sonorous and rhythmically sensual use of words. His poetry is rarely abstract, and the vivid, descriptive imagery and the narrative form of verse he favored make it easy to read and follow. His subject matter touched on American life and its verities, be it legendary heroism as in "Paul Revere's Ride" or in the honest, upright, and hard-working man of "The Village Blacksmith."

This collection brings together Longfellow's best and most famous poems, providing a complete overview of his versatile and multifaceted genius. All the classic Longfellow selections, including "A Psalm of Life," "The Children's Hour," and "The Day Is Done," are here, as well as lesser-known but equally worthy poems, like "The Cross of Snow," a sonnet written in memory of his second wife who died tragically in a fire. Also included, in their entirety, are his two long narrative masterpieces, *Evangeline* and *The Courtship of Miles Standish*.

CHRISTOPHER MOORE

New York
1992

Shorter Lyric
and
Narrative Poems

BURIAL OF THE MINNISINK

On sunny slope and beechen swell,
The shadowed light of evening fell;
And, where the maple's leaf was brown,
With soft and silent lapse came down,
The glory, that the wood receives,
At sunset, in its golden leaves.

Far upward in the mellow light
Rose the blue hills. One cloud of white,
Around a far uplifted cone,
In the warm blush of evening shone;
An image of the silver lakes,
By which the Indian's soul awakes.

But soon a funeral hymn was heard
Where the soft breath of evening stirred
The tall, gray forest; and a band
Of stern in heart, and strong in hand,
Came winding down beside the wave,
To lay the red chief in his grave.

They sang, that by his native bowers
He stood, in the last moon of flowers,
And thirty snows had not yet shed
Their glory on the warrior's head;
But, as the summer fruit decays,
So died he in those naked days.

A dark cloak of the roebuck's skin
Covered the warrior, and within
Its heavy folds the weapons, made
For the hard toils of war, were laid;

The cuirass, woven of plaited reeds,
And the broad belt of shells and beads.

Before, a dark-haired virgin train
Chanted the death dirge of the slain;
Behind, the long procession came
Of hoary men and chiefs of fame,
With heavy hearts, and eyes of grief,
Leading the warhorse of their chief.

Stripped of his proud and martial dress,
Uncurbed, unreined, and riderless,
With darting eye, and nostril spread,
And heavy and impatient tread,
He came; and oft that eye so proud
Asked for his rider in the crowd.

They buried the dark chief; they freed
Beside the grave his battle steed;
And swift an arrow cleaved its way
To his stern heart! One piercing neigh
'Arose, and, on the dead man's plain,
The rider grasps his steed again.

A PSALM OF LIFE

Tell me not, in mournful numbers,
    Life is but an empty dream!—
For the soul is dead that slumbers,
    And things are not what they seem.

Life is real! Life is earnest!
    And the grave is not its goal;
Dust thou art, to dust returnest,
    Was not spoken of the soul.

Not enjoyment, and not sorrow,
    Is our destined end or way;
But to act, that each tomorrow
    Find us farther than today.

Art is long, and Time is fleeting,
    And our hearts, though stout and brave,
Still, like muffled drums, are beating
    Funeral marches to the grave.

In the world's broad field of battle,
    In the bivouac of Life,
Be not like dumb, driven cattle!
    Be a hero in the strife!

Trust no Future, howe'er pleasant!
    Let the dead Past bury its dead!
Act,—act in the living Present!
    Heart within, and God o'erhead!

Lives of great men all remind us
  We can make our lives sublime,
And, departing, leave behind us
  Footprints on the sands of time;

Footprints, that perhaps another,
  Sailing o'er life's solemn main,
A forlorn and shipwrecked brother,
  Seeing, shall take heart again.

Let us, then, be up and doing,
  With a heart for any fate;
Still achieving, still pursuing,
  Learn to labor and to wait.

HYMN TO THE NIGHT

I heard the trailing garments of the Night
    Sweep through her marble halls!
I saw her sable skirts all fringed with light
    From the celestial walls!

I felt her presence, by its spell of might,
    Stoop o'er me from above;
The calm, majestic presence of the Night,
    As of the one I love.

I heard the sounds of sorrow and delight,
    The manifold, soft chimes,
That fill the haunted chambers of the Night,
    Like some old poet's rhymes.

From the cool cisterns of the midnight air
    My spirit drank repose;
The fountain of perpetual peace flows there,—
    From those deep cisterns flows.

O holy Night! from thee I learn to bear
    What man has borne before!
Thou layest thy finger on the lips of Care,
    And they complain no more.

Peace! Peace! Orestes-like I breathe this prayer!
    Descend with broad-winged flight,
The welcome, the thrice-prayed for, the most fair,
    The best-beloved Night!

THE WRECK OF THE HESPERUS

It was the schooner Hesperus,
   That sailed the wintry sea;
And the skipper had taken his little daughter,
   To bear him company.

Blue were her eyes as the fairy-flax,
   Her cheeks like the dawn of day,
And her bosom white as the hawthorn buds,
   That ope in the month of May.

The skipper he stood beside the helm,
   His pipe was in his mouth,
And he watched how the veering flaw did blow
   The smoke now West, now South.

Then up and spake an old sailor,
   Had sailed to the Spanish Main,
"I pray thee, put into yonder port,
   For I fear a hurricane.

"Last night, the moon had a golden ring,
   And tonight no moon we see!"
The skipper, he blew a whiff from his pipe,
   And a scornful laugh laughed he.

Colder and louder blew the wind,
   A gale from the Northeast,
The snow fell hissing in the brine,
   And the billows frothed like yeast.

Down came the storm, and smote amain
   The vessel in its strength;
She shuddered and paused, like a frighted steed,
   Then leaped her cable's length.

"Come hither! come hither! my little daughter,
   And do not tremble so;
For I can weather the roughest gale
   That ever wind did blow."

He wrapped her warm in his seaman's coat
   Against the stinging blast;
He cut a rope from a broken spar,
   And bound her to the mast.

"O father! I hear the churchbells ring,
   Oh say, what may it be?"
" 'T is a fog-bell on a rock-bound coast!"—
   And he steered for the open sea.

"O father! I hear the sound of guns,
   Oh say, what may it be?"
"Some ship in distress, that cannot live
   In such an angry sea!"

"O father! I see a gleaming light,
   Oh say, what may it be?"
But the father answered never a word,
   A frozen corpse was he.

Lashed to the helm, all stiff and stark,
   With his face turned to the skies,
The lantern gleamed through the gleaming snow
   On his fixed and glassy eyes.

Then the maiden clasped her hands and prayed
    That saved she might be;
And she thought of Christ, who stilled the wave,
    On the Lake of Galilee.

And fast through the midnight dark and drear,
    Through the whistling sleet and snow,
Like a sheeted ghost, the vessel swept
    Tow'rds the reef of Norman's Woe.

And ever the fitful gusts between
    A sound came from the land;
It was the sound of the trampling surf
    On the rocks and the hard sea-sand.

The breakers were right beneath her bows,
    She drifted a dreary wreck,
And a whooping billow swept the crew
    Like icicles from her deck.

She struck where the white and fleecy waves
    Looked soft as carded wool,
But the cruel rocks, they gored her side
    Like the horns of an angry bull.

Her rattling shrouds, all sheathed in ice,
    With the masts went by the board;
Like a vessel of glass, she stove and sank,
    Ho! ho! the breakers roared!

At daybreak, on the bleak sea-beach,
    A fisherman stood aghast,
To see the form of a maiden fair,
    Lashed close to a drifting mast.

The salt sea was frozen on her breast,
    The salt tears in her eyes;
And he saw her hair, like the brown seaweed,
    On the billows fall and rise.

Such was the wreck of the Hesperus,
    In the midnight and the snow!
Christ save us all from a death like this,
    On the reef of Norman's Woe!

THE VILLAGE BLACKSMITH

Under a spreading chestnut tree
  The village smithy stands;
The smith, a mighty man is he,
  With large and sinewy hands;
And the muscles of his brawny arms
  Are strong as iron bands.

His hair is crisp, and black, and long,
  His face is like the tan;
His brow is wet with honest sweat,
  He earns whate'er he can,
And looks the whole world in the face,
  For he owes not any man.

Week in, week out, from morn till night,
  You can hear his bellows blow;
You can hear him swing his heavy sledge,
  With measured beat and slow,
Like a sexton ringing the village bell,
  When the evening sun is low.

And children coming home from school
  Look in at the open door;
They love to see the flaming forge,
  And hear the bellows roar,
And catch the burning sparks that fly
  Like chaff from a threshing-floor.

He goes on Sunday to the church,
   And sits among his boys;
He hears the parson pray and preach,
   He hears his daughter's voice,
Singing in the village choir,
   And it makes his heart rejoice.

It sounds to him like her mother's voice,
   Singing in Paradise!
He needs must think of her once more,
   How in the grave she lies;
And with his hard, rough hand he wipes
   A tear out of his eyes.

Toiling,—rejoicing,—sorrowing,
   Onward through life he goes;
Each morning sees some task begin,
   Each evening sees it close;
Something attempted, something done,
   Has earned a night's repose.

Thanks, thanks to thee, my worthy friend,
   For the lesson thou hast taught!
Thus at the flaming forge of life
   Our fortunes must be wrought;
Thus on its sounding anvil shaped
   Each burning deed and thought.

EXCELSIOR

The shades of night were falling fast,
As through an Alpine village passed
A youth, who bore, 'mid snow and ice,
A banner with the strange device,
　　　　Excelsior!

His brow was sad; his eye beneath
Flashed like a falchion from its sheath,
And like a silver clarion rung
The accents of that unknown tongue,
　　　　Excelsior!

In happy homes he saw the light
Of household fires gleam warm and bright;
Above, the spectral glaciers shone,
And from his lips escaped a groan,
　　　　Excelsior!

"Try not the Pass!" the old man said;
"Dark lowers the tempest overhead,
The roaring torrent is deep and wide!"
And loud that clarion voice replied,
　　　　Excelsior!

"O stay," the maiden said, "and rest
Thy weary head upon this breast!"
A tear stood in his bright blue eye,
But still he answered, with a sigh,
　　　　Excelsior!

"Beware the pine tree's withered branch!
Beware the awful avalanche!"
This was the peasant's last Goodnight.
A voice replied, far up the height,
        Excelsior!

At break of day, as heavenward
The pious monks of Saint Bernard
Uttered the oft-repeated prayer,
A voice cried through the startled air,
        Excelsior!

A traveller, by the faithful hound,
Half-buried in the snow was found,
Still grasping in his hand of ice
That banner with the strange device,
        Excelsior!

There in the twilight cold and gray,
Lifeless, but beautiful, he lay,
And from the sky, serene and far,
A voice fell, like a falling star,
        Excelsior!

THE WITNESSES

In Ocean's wide domains,
  Half buried in the sands,
Lie skeletons in chains,
  With shackled feet and hands.

Beyond the fall of dews,
  Deeper than plummet lies,
Float ships, with all their crews,
  No more to sink nor rise.

There the black Slave-ship swims,
  Freighted with human forms,
Whose fettered, fleshless limbs
  Are not the sport of storms.

These are the bones of Slaves;
  They gleam from the abyss;
They cry, from yawning waves,
  "We are the Witnesses!"

Within Earth's wide domains
  Are markets for men's lives;
Their necks are galled with chains,
  Their wrists are cramped with gyves.

Dead bodies, that the kite
  In deserts makes its prey;
Murders, that with affright
  Scare schoolboys from their play!

All evil thoughts and deeds;
  Anger, and lust, and pride;
The foulest, rankest weeds,
  That choke Life's groaning tide!

These are the woes of Slaves;
  They glare from the abyss;
They cry, from unknown graves,
  "We are the Witnesses!"

THE SLAVE SINGING
AT MIDNIGHT

Loud he sang the psalm of David!
He, a Negro and enslaved,
Sang of Israel's victory,
Sang of Zion, bright and free.

In that hour, when night is calmest,
Sang he from the Hebrew Psalmist,
In a voice so sweet and clear
That I could not choose but hear,

Songs of triumph, and ascriptions,
Such as reached the swart Egyptians,
When upon the Red Sea coast
Perished Pharaoh and his host.

And the voice of his devotion
Filled my soul with strange emotion;
For its tones by turns were glad,
Sweetly solemn, wildly sad.

Paul and Silas, in their prison,
Sang of Christ, the Lord arisen,
And an earthquake's arm of might
Broke their dungeon gates at night.

But, alas! what holy angel
Brings the Slave this glad evangel?
And what earthquake's arm of might
Breaks his dungeon gates at night?

THE WARNING

Beware! The Israelite of old, who tore
   The lion in his path,—when, poor and blind,
He saw the blessed light of heaven no more,
   Shorn of his noble strength and forced to grind
In prison, and at last led forth to be
A pander to Philistine revelry,—

Upon the pillars of the temple laid
   His desperate hands, and in its overthrow
Destroyed himself, and with him those who made
   A cruel mockery of his sightless woe;
The poor, blind Slave, the scoff and jest of all,
Expired, and thousands perished in the fall!

There is a poor, blind Samson in this land,
   Shorn of his strength and bound in bonds of steel,
Who may, in some grim revel, raise his hand,
   And shake the pillars of this Commonweal,
Till the vast Temple of our liberties
A shapeless mass of wreck and rubbish lies.

THE BELFRY OF BRUGES

In the marketplace of Bruges stands the belfry old and
  brown;
Thrice consumed and thrice rebuilded, still it watches o'er
  the town.

As the summer morn was breaking, on that lofty tower I
  stood,
And the world threw off the darkness, like the weeds of
  widowhood.

Thick with towns and hamlets studded, and with streams
  and vapors gray,
Like a shield embossed with silver, round and vast the
  landscape lay.

At my feet the city slumbered. From its chimneys, here
  and there,
Wreaths of snow-white smoke, ascending, vanished, ghost-
  like, into air.

Not a sound rose from the city at that early morning hour,
But I heard a heart of iron beating in the ancient tower.

From their nests beneath the rafters sang the swallows wild
  and high;
And the world, beneath me sleeping, seemed more distant
  than the sky.

Then most musical and solemn, bringing back the olden
  times,
With their strange, unearthly changes rang the melancholy
  chimes,

Like the psalms from some old cloister, when the nuns
    sing in the choir;
And the great bell tolled among them, like the chanting of
    a friar.

Visions of the days departed, shadowy phantoms filled my
    brain;
They who live in history only seemed to walk the earth
    again;

All the Foresters of Flanders,—mighty Baldwin Bras de
    Fer,
Lyderick du Bucq and Cressy, Philip, Guy de Dampierre.

I beheld the pageants splendid that adorned those days
    of old;
Stately dames, like queens attended, knights who bore
    the Fleece of Gold;

Lombard and Venetian merchants with deep-laden
    argosies;
Ministers from twenty nations; more than royal pomp and
    ease.

I beheld proud Maximilian, kneeling humbly on the
    ground;
I beheld the gentle Mary, hunting with her hawk and
    hound;

And her lighted bridal-chamber, where a duke slept with
    the queen,
And the armed guard around them, and the sword un-
    sheathed between.

I beheld the Flemish weavers, with Namur and Juliers
bold,
Marching homeward from the bloody battle of the Spurs
of Gold;

Saw the fight at Minnewater, saw the White Hoods moving
west,
Saw great Artevelde victorious scale the Golden Dragon's
nest.

And again the whiskered Spaniard all the land with terror
smote;
And again the wild alarum sounded from the tocsin's
throat;

Till the bell of Ghent responded o'er lagoon and dike of
sand,
"I am Roland! I am Roland! there is victory in the land!"

Then the sound of drums aroused me. The awakened city's
roar
Chased the phantoms I had summoned back into their
graves once more.

Hours had passed away like minutes; and, before I was
aware,
Lo! the shadow of the belfry crossed the sun-illumined
square.

MEZZO CAMMIN

Half of my life is gone, and I have let
 The years slip from me and have not fulfilled
 The aspiration of my youth, to build
 Some tower of song with lofty parapet.
Not indolence, nor pleasure, nor the fret
 Of restless passions that would not be stilled,
 But sorrow, and a care that almost killed,
 Kept me from what I may accomplish yet;
Though, halfway up the hill, I see the Past
 Lying beneath me with its sounds and sights,—
 A city in the twilight dim and vast,
With smoking roofs, soft bells, and gleaming lights,—
 And hear above me on the autumnal blast
 The cataract of Death far thundering from the heights.

THE ARSENAL AT SPRINGFIELD

This is the Arsenal. From floor to ceiling,
  Like a huge organ, rise the burnished arms;
But from their silent pipes no anthem pealing
  Startles the villages with strange alarms.

Ah! what a sound will rise, how wild and dreary,
  When the death-angel touches those swift keys!
What loud lament and dismal Miserere
  Will mingle with their awful symphonies!

I hear even now the infinite fierce chorus,
  The cries of agony, the endless groan,
Which, through the ages that have gone before us,
  In long reverberations reach our own.

On helm and harness rings the Saxon hammer,
  Through Cimbric forest roars the Norseman's song,
And loud, amid the universal clamor,
  O'er distant deserts sounds the Tartar gong.

I hear the Florentine, who from his palace
  Wheels out his battle-bell with dreadful din,
And Aztec priests upon their teocallis
  Beat the wild war-drums made of serpent's skin;

The tumult of each sacked and burning village;
  The shout that every prayer for mercy drowns;
The soldiers' revels in the midst of pillage;
  The wail of famine in beleaguered towns;

The bursting shell, the gateway wrenched asunder,
    The rattling musketry, the clashing blade;
And ever and anon, in tones of thunder
    The diapason of the cannonade.

Is it, O man, with such discordant noises,
    With such accursed instruments as these,
Thou drownest Nature's sweet and kindly voices,
    And jarrest the celestial harmonies?

Were half the power, that fills the world with terror,
    Were half the wealth bestowed on camps and courts,
Given to redeem the human mind from error,
    There were no need of arsenals or forts:

The warrior's name would be a name abhorrèd!
    And every nation, that should lift again
Its hand against a brother, on its forehead
    Would wear for evermore the curse of Cain!

Down the dark future, through long generations,
    The echoing sounds grow fainter and then cease;
And like a bell, with solemn, sweet vibrations,
    I hear once more the voice of Christ say, "Peace!"

Peace! and no longer from its brazen portals
    The blast of War's great organ shakes the skies!
But beautiful as songs of the immortals,
    The holy melodies of love arise.

SEAWEED

When descends on the Atlantic
   The gigantic
Storm-wind of the equinox,
Landward in his wrath he scourges
   The toiling surges,
Laden with seaweed from the rocks:

From Bermuda's reefs; from edges
   Of sunken ledges,
In some far-off, bright Azore;
From Bahama, and the dashing,
   Silver-flashing
Surges of San Salvador;

From the tumbling surf, that buries
   The Orkneyan skerries,
Answering the hoarse Hebrides;
And from wrecks of ships, and drifting
   Spars, uplifting
On the desolate, rainy seas;—

Ever drifting, drifting, drifting,
   On the shifting
Currents of the restless main;
Till in sheltered coves, and reaches
   Of sandy beaches,
All have found repose again.

So when storms of wild emotion
   Strike the ocean
Of the poet's soul, erelong
From each cave and rocky fastness,
   In its vastness,
Floats some fragment of a song:

From the far-off isles enchanted,
   Heaven has planted
With the golden fruit of Truth;
From the flashing surf, whose vision
   Gleams Elysian
In the tropic clime of Youth;

From the strong Will, and the Endeavor
   That forever
Wrestle with the tides of Fate;
From the wreck of Hopes far-scattered,
   Tempest-shattered,
Floating waste and desolate;—

Ever drifting, drifting, drifting
   On the shifting
Currents of the restless heart;
Till at length in books recorded,
   They, like hoarded
Household words, no more depart.

THE DAY IS DONE

The day is done, and the darkness
 Falls from the wings of Night,
As a feather is wafted downward
 From an eagle in his flight.

I see the lights of the village
 Gleam through the rain and the mist,
And a feeling of sadness comes o'er me
 That my soul cannot resist:

A feeling of sadness and longing,
 That is not akin to pain,
And resembles sorrow only
 As the mist resembles the rain.

Come, read to me some poem,
 Some simple and heartfelt lay,
That shall soothe this restless feeling,
 And banish the thoughts of day.

Not from the grand old masters,
 Not from the bards sublime,
Whose distant footsteps echo
 Through the corridors of Time.

For, like strains of martial music,
 Their mighty thoughts suggest
Life's endless toil and endeavor;
 And tonight I long for rest.

Read from some humbler poet,
  Whose songs gushed from his heart,
As showers from the clouds of summer,
  Or tears from the eyelids start;

Who, through long days of labor,
  And nights devoid of ease,
Still heard in his soul the music
  Of wonderful melodies.

Such songs have power to quiet
  The restless pulse of care,
And come like the benediction
  That follows after prayer.

Then read from the treasured volume
  The poem of thy choice,
And lend to the rhyme of the poet
  The beauty of thy voice.

And the night shall be filled with music,
  And the cares, that infest the day,
Shall fold their tents, like the Arabs,
  And as silently steal away.

THE OLD CLOCK ON THE STAIRS

Somewhat back from the village street
Stands the old-fashioned country seat.
Across its antique portico
Tall poplar trees their shadows throw;
And from its station in the hall
An ancient timepiece says to all,—
     "Forever—never!
     Never—forever!"

Halfway up the stairs it stands,
And points and beckons with its hands
From its case of massive oak,
Like a monk, who, under his cloak,
Crosses himself, and sighs, alas!
With sorrowful voice to all who pass,—
     "Forever—never!
     Never—forever!"

By day its voice is low and light;
But in the silent dead of night,
Distinct as a passing footstep's fall,
It echoes along the vacant hall,
Along the ceiling, along the floor,
And seems to say, at each chamber door,—
     "Forever—never!
     Never—forever!"

Through days of sorrow and of mirth,
Through days of death and days of birth,
Throughout every swift vicissitude
Of changeful time, unchanged it has stood,

And as if, like God, it all things saw,
It calmly repeats those words of awe,—
      "Forever—never!
      Never—forever!"

In that mansion used to be
Free hearted Hospitality;
His great fires up the chimney roared;
The stranger feasted at his board;
But, like the skeleton at the feast,
That warning timepiece never ceased,—
      "Forever—never!
      Never—forever!"

There groups of merry children played,
There youths and maidens dreaming strayed;
O precious hours! O golden prime,
And affluence of love and time!
Even as a miser counts his gold,
Those hours the ancient timepiece told,—
      "Forever—never!
      Never—forever!"

From that chamber, clothed in white,
The bride came forth on her wedding night;
There, in that silent room below,
The dead lay in his shroud of snow;
And in the hush that followed the prayer,
Was heard the old clock on the stair,—
      "Forever—never!
      Never—forever!"

All are scattered now and fled,
Some are married, some are dead;

And when I ask, with throbs of pain,
"Ah! when shall they all meet again?"
As in the days long since gone by,
The ancient timepiece makes reply,—
      "Forever—never!
      Never—forever!"

Never here, forever there,
Where all parting, pain, and care,
And death, and time shall disappear,—
Forever there, but never here!
The horologe of Eternity
Sayeth this incessantly,—
      "Forever—never!
      Never—forever!"

THE ARROW AND THE SONG

I shot an arrow into the air,
It fell to earth, I knew not where;
For, so swiftly it flew, the sight
Could not follow it in its flight.

I breathed a song into the air,
It fell to earth, I knew not where;
For who has sight so keen and strong
That it can follow the flight of song?

Long, long afterward, in an oak
I found the arrow, still unbroke;
And the song, from beginning to end,
I found again in the heart of a friend.

THE FIRE OF DRIFTWOOD

DEVEREUX FARM, NEAR MARBLEHEAD

We sat within the farmhouse old,
  Whose windows, looking o'er the bay,
Gave to the sea breeze damp and cold,
  An easy entrance, night and day.

Not far away we saw the port,
  The strange, old-fashioned, silent town,
The lighthouse, the dismantled fort,
  The wooden houses, quaint and brown.

We sat and talked until the night,
  Descending, filled the little room;
Our faces faded from the sight,
  Our voices only broke the gloom.

We spake of many a vanished scene,
  Of what we once had thought and said,
Of what had been, and might have been,
  And who was changed, and who was dead;

And all that fills the hearts of friends,
  When first they feel, with secret pain,
Their lives thenceforth have separate ends,
  And never can be one again;

The first slight swerving of the heart,
  That words are powerless to express,
And leave it still unsaid in part,
  Or say it in too great excess.

The very tones in which we spake
 Had something strange, I could but mark;
The leaves of memory seemed to make
 A mournful rustling in the dark.

Oft died the words upon our lips,
 As suddenly, from out the fire
Built of the wreck of stranded ships,
 The flames would leap and then expire.

And, as their splendor flashed and failed,
 We thought of wrecks upon the main,
Of ships dismasted, that were hailed
 And sent no answer back again.

The windows, rattling in their frames,
 The ocean, roaring up the beach,
The gusty blast, the bickering flames,
 All mingled vaguely in our speech;

Until they made themselves a part
 Of fancies floating through the brain,
The long-lost ventures of the heart,
 That send no answers back again.

O flames that glowed! O hearts that yearned!
 They were indeed too much akin,
The driftwood fire without that burned,
 The thoughts that burned and glowed within.

HAUNTED HOUSES

All houses wherein men have lived and died
 Are haunted houses. Through the open doors
The harmless phantoms on their errands glide,
 With feet that make no sound upon the floors.

We meet them at the doorway, on the stair,
 Along the passages they come and go,
Impalpable impressions on the air,
 A sense of something moving to and fro.

There are more guests at table than the hosts
 Invited; the illuminated hall
Is thronged with quiet, inoffensive ghosts,
 As silent as the pictures on the wall.

The stranger at my fireside cannot see
 The forms I see, nor hear the sounds I hear;
He but perceives what is; while unto me
 All that has been is visible and clear.

We have no title deeds to house or lands;
 Owners and occupants of earlier dates
From graves forgotten stretch their dusty hands,
 And hold in mortmain still their old estates.

The spirit-world around this world of sense
 Floats like an atmosphere, and everywhere
Wafts through these earthly mists and vapors dense
 A vital breath of more ethereal air.

Our little lives are kept in equipoise
        By opposite attractions and desires;
The struggle of the instinct that enjoys,
        And the more noble instinct that aspires.

These perturbations, this perpetual jar
        Of earthly wants and aspirations high,
Come from the influence of an unseen star,
        An undiscovered planet in our sky.

And as the moon from some dark gate of cloud
        Throws o'er the sea a floating bridge of light,
Across whose trembling planks our fancies crowd
        Into the realm of mystery and night,—

So from the world of spirits there descends
        A bridge of light, connecting it with this,
O'er whose unsteady floor, that sways and bends,
        Wander our thoughts above the dark abyss.

IN THE CHURCHYARD
AT CAMBRIDGE

In the village churchyard she lies,
Dust is in her beautiful eyes,
    No more she breathes, nor feels, nor stirs;
At her feet and at her head
Lies a slave to attend the dead,
    But their dust is white as hers.

Was she, a lady of high degree,
So much in love with the vanity
    And foolish pomp of this world of ours?
Or was it Christian charity,
And lowliness and humility,
    The richest and rarest of all dowers?

Who shall tell us? No one speaks;
No color shoots into those cheeks,
    Either of anger or of pride,
At the rude question we have asked;
Nor will the mystery be unmasked
    By those who are sleeping at her side.

Hereafter?—And do you think to look
On the terrible pages of that Book
    To find her failings, faults, and errors?
Ah, you will then have other cares,
In your own shortcomings and despairs,
    In your own secret sins and terrors!

THE JEWISH CEMETERY AT NEWPORT

How strange it seems! These Hebrews in their graves,
 Close by the street of this fair seaport town,
Silent beside the never-silent waves,
 At rest in all this moving up and down!

The trees are white with dust, that o'er their sleep
 Wave their broad curtains in the south wind's breath,
While underneath these leafy tents they keep
 The long, mysterious Exodus of Death.

And these sepulchral stones, so old and brown,
 That pave with level flags their burial-place,
Seem like the tablets of the Law, thrown down
 And broken by Moses at the mountain's base.

The very names recorded here are strange,
 Of foreign accent, and of different climes;
Alvares and Rivera interchange
 With Abraham and Jacob of old times.

"Blessed be God! for he created Death!"
 The mourners said, "and Death is rest and peace;"
Then added, in the certainty of faith,
 "And giveth Life that nevermore shall cease."

Closed are the portals of their Synagogue,
 No Psalms of David now the silence break,
No Rabbi reads the ancient Decalogue
 In the grand dialect the Prophets spake.

Gone are the living, but the dead remain,
 And not neglected; for a hand unseen,

Scattering its bounty, like a summer rain,
   Still keeps their graves and their remembrance green.

How came they here? What burst of Christian hate,
   What persecution, merciless and blind,
Drove o'er the sea—that desert desolate—
   These Ishmaels and Hagars of mankind?

They lived in narrow streets and lanes obscure,
   Ghetto and Judenstrass, in mirk and mire;
Taught in the school of patience to endure
   The life of anguish and the death of fire.

All their lives long, with the unleavened bread
   And bitter herbs of exile and its fears,
The wasting famine of the heart they fed,
   And slaked its thirst with marah of their tears.

Anathema maranatha! was the cry
   That rang from town to town, from street to street;
At every gate the accursed Mordecai
   Was mocked and jeered, and spurned by Christian
      feet.

Pride and humiliation hand in hand
   Walked with them through the world where'er they
      went;
Trampled and beaten were they as the sand,
   And yet unshaken as the continent.

For in the background figures vague and vast
   Of patriarchs and of prophets rose sublime,
And all the great traditions of the Past
   They saw reflected in the coming time.

And thus forever with reverted look
The mystic volume of the world they read,
Spelling it backward, like a Hebrew book,
Till life became a Legend of the Dead.

But ah! what once has been shall be no more!
The groaning earth in travail and in pain
Brings forth its races, but does not restore,
And the dead nations never rise again.

MY LOST YOUTH

Often I think of the beautiful town
   That is seated by the sea;
Often in thought go up and down
The pleasant streets of that dear old town,
   And my youth comes back to me.
     And a verse of a Lapland song
     Is haunting my memory still:
"A boy's will is the wind's will,
And the thoughts of youth are long, long thoughts."

I can see the shadowy lines of its trees,
   And catch, in sudden gleams,
The sheen of the far-surrounding seas,
And islands that were the Hesperides
   Of all my boyish dreams.
     And the burden of that old song,
     It murmurs and whispers still:
"A boy's will is the wind's will,
And the thoughts of youth are long, long thoughts."

I remember the black wharves and the slips,
   And the sea-tides tossing free;
And Spanish sailors with bearded lips,
And the beauty and mystery of the ships,
   And the magic of the sea.
     And the voice of that wayward song
     Is singing and saying still:
A boy's will is the wind's will,
And the thoughts of youth are long, long thoughts."

I remember the bulwarks by the shore,
   And the fort upon the hill;

The sunrise gun, with its hollow roar,
The drum-beat repeated o'er and o'er,
　　And the bugle wild and shrill.
　　　　And the music of that old song
　　　　Throbs in my memory still:
　　"A boy's will is the wind's will,
And the thoughts of youth are long, long thoughts."

I remember the sea-fight far away,
　　How it thundered o'er the tide!
And the dead captains, as they lay
In their graves, o'erlooking the tranquil bay,
　　Where they in battle died.
　　　　And the sound of that mournful song
　　　　Goes through me with a thrill:
　　"A boy's will is the wind's will,
And the thoughts of youth are long, long thoughts."

I can see the breezy dome of groves,
　　The shadows of Deering's Woods;
And the friendships old and the early loves
Come back with a Sabbath sound, as of doves
　　In quiet neighborhoods.
　　　　And the verse of that sweet old song,
　　　　It flutters and murmurs still:
　　"A boy's will is the wind's will,
And the thoughts of youth are long, long thoughts."

I remember the gleams and glooms that dart
　　Across the schoolboy's brain;
The song and the silence in the heart,
That in part are prophecies, and in part
　　Are longings wild and vain.
　　　　And the voice of that fitful song
　　　　Sings on, and is never still:

"A boy's will is the wind's will,
And the thoughts of youth are long, long thoughts."

There are things of which I may not speak;
   There are dreams that cannot die;
There are thoughts that make the strong heart weak,
And bring pallor into the cheek,
   And a mist before the eye.
      And the words of that fatal song
      Come over me like a chill:
"A boy's will is the wind's will,
And the thoughts of youth are long, long thoughts."

Strange to me now are the forms I meet
   When I visit the dear old town;
But the native air is pure and sweet,
And the trees that o'ershadow each well-known street,
   As they balance up and down,
      Are singing the beautiful song,
      Are sighing and whispering still:
"A boy's will is the wind's will,
And the thoughts of youth are long, long thoughts."

And Deering's Woods are fresh and fair,
   And with joy that is almost pain
My heart goes back to wander there,
And among the dreams of the days that were,
   I find my lost youth again.
      And the strange and beautiful song,
      The groves are repeating it still:
"A boy's will is the wind's will,
And the thoughts of youth are long, long thoughts."

SNOWFLAKES

Out of the bosom of the Air,
  Out of the cloud-folds of her garments shaken,
Over the woodlands brown and bare,
  Over the harvest-fields forsaken,
    Silent, and soft, and slow
    Descends the snow.

Even as our cloudy fancies take
  Suddenly shape in some divine expression,
Even as the troubled heart doth make
  In the white countenance confession,
    The troubled sky reveals
    The grief it feels.

This is the poem of the air,
  Slowly in silent syllables recorded;
This is the secret of despair,
  Long in its cloudy bosom hoarded,
    Now whispered and revealed
    To wood and field.

THE CHILDREN'S HOUR

Between the dark and the daylight,
   When the night is beginning to lower,
Comes a pause in the day's occupations,
   That is known as the Children's Hour.

I hear in the chamber above me
   The patter of little feet,
The sound of a door that is opened,
   And voices soft and sweet.

From my study I see in the lamplight,
   Descending the broad hall stair,
Grave Alice, and laughing Allegra,
   And Edith with golden hair.

A whisper, and then a silence:
   Yet I know by their merry eyes
They are plotting and planning together
   To take me by surprise.

A sudden rush from the stairway,
   A sudden raid from the hall!
By three doors left unguarded
   They enter my castle wall!

They climb up into my turret
   O'er the arms and back of my chair;
If I try to escape, they surround me;
   They seem to be everywhere.

They almost devour me with kisses,
  Their arms about me entwine,
Till I think of the Bishop of Bingen
  In his Mouse-Tower on the Rhine!

Do you think, O blue-eyed banditti,
  Because you have scaled the wall,
Such an old mustache as I am
  Is not a match for you all!

I have you fast in my fortress,
  And will not let you depart,
But put you down into the dungeon
  In the round-tower of my heart.

And there will I keep you forever,
  Yes, forever and a day,
Till the walls shall crumble to ruin,
  And moulder in dust away!

THE BELLS OF LYNN

HEARD AT NAHANT

O curfew of the setting sun! O Bells of Lynn!
O requiem of the dying day! O Bells of Lynn!

From the dark belfries of yon cloud-cathedral wafted,
Your sounds aerial seem to float, O Bells of Lynn!

Borne on the evening wind across the crimson twilight,
O'er land and sea they rise and fall, O Bells of Lynn!

The fisherman in his boat, far out beyond the headland,
Listens, and leisurely rows ashore, O Bells of Lynn!

Over the shining sands the wandering cattle homeward
Follow each other at your call, O Bells of Lynn!

The distant lighthouse hears, and with his flaming signal
Answers you, passing the watchword on, O Bells of Lynn!

And down the darkening coast run the tumultuous surges,
And clap their hands, and shout to you, O Bells of Lynn!

Till from the shuddering sea, with your wild incantations,
Ye summon up the spectral moon, O Bells of Lynn!

And startled at the sight, like the weird woman of Endor,
Ye cry aloud, and then are still, O Bells of Lynn!

PAUL REVERE'S RIDE

Listen, my children, and you shall hear
Of the midnight ride of Paul Revere,
On the eighteenth of April, in Seventy-five;
Hardly a man is now alive
Who remembers that famous day and year.

He said to his friend, "If the British march
By land or sea from the town tonight,
Hang a lantern aloft in the belfry arch
Of the North Church tower as a signal light,—
One, if by land, and two, if by sea;
And I on the opposite shore will be,
Ready to ride and spread the alarm
Through every Middlesex village and farm,
For the country folk to be up and to arm"
Then he said, "Good-night!" and with muffled oar
Silently rowed to the Charlestown shore,
Just as the moon rose over the bay,
Where swinging wide at her moorings lay
The Somerset, British man-of-war;
A phantom ship, with each mast and spar
Across the moon like a prison bar,
And a huge black hulk, that was magnified
By its own reflection in the tide.
Meanwhile, his friend, through alley and street,
Wanders and watches with eager ears,
Till in the silence around him he hears
The muster of men at the barrack door,
The sound of arms, and the tramp of feet,
And the measured tread of the grenadiers,
Marching down to their boats on the shore.

Then he climbed the tower of the Old North Church,
By the wooden stairs, with stealthy tread,
To the belfry-chamber overhead,
And startled the pigeons from their perch
On the somber rafters, that round him made
Masses and moving shapes of shade,—
By the trembling ladder, steep and tall,
To the highest window in the wall,
Where he paused to listen and look down
A moment on the roofs of the town,
And the moonlight flowing over all.
Beneath, in the churchyard, lay the dead,
In their night-encampment on the hill,
Wrapped in silence so deep and still
That he could hear, like a sentinel's tread,
The watchful night wind, as it went
Creeping along from tent to tent,
And seeming to whisper, "All is well!"
A moment only he feels the spell
Of the place and the hour, and the secret dread
Of the lonely belfry and the dead;
For suddenly all his thoughts are bent
On a shadowy something far away,
Where the river widens to meet the bay,—
A line of black that bends and floats
On the rising tide, like a bridge of boats.

Meanwhile, impatient to mount and ride,
Booted and spurred, with a heavy stride
On the opposite shore walked Paul Revere.
Now he patted his horse's side,
Now gazed at the landscape far and near,
Then, impetuous, stamped the earth,
And turned and tightened his saddle-girth;
But mostly he watched with eager search
The belfry-tower of the Old North Church,

As it rose above the graves on the hill,
Lonely and spectral and somber and still.
And lo! as he looks, on the belfry's height
A glimmer, and then a gleam of light!
He springs to the saddle, the bridle he turns,
But lingers and gazes, till full on his sight
A second lamp in the belfry burns!
A hurry of hoofs in a village street,
A shape in the moonlight, a bulk in the dark,
And beneath, from the pebbles, in passing, a spark
Struck out by a steed flying fearless and fleet:
That was all! And yet, through the gloom and the light,
The fate of a nation was riding that night;
And the spark struck out by that steed, in his flight,
Kindled the land into flame with its heat.
He has left the village and mounted the steep,
And beneath him, tranquil and broad and deep,
Is the Mystic, meeting the ocean tides;
And under the alders, that skirt its edge,
Now soft on the sand, now loud on the ledge,
Is heard the tramp of his steed as he rides.

It was twelve by the village clock,
When he crossed the bridge into Medford town.
He heard the crowing of the cock,
And the barking of the farmer's dog,
And felt the damp of the river fog,
That rises after the sun goes down.
It was one by the village clock,
When he galloped into Lexington.
He saw the gilded weathercock
Swim in the moonlight as he passed,
And the meeting-house windows, blank and bare,
Gaze at him with a spectral glare,
As if they already stood aghast
At the bloody work they would look upon.

It was two by the village clock,
When he came to the bridge in Concord town.
He heard the bleating of the flock,
And the twitter of birds among the trees,
And felt the breath of the morning breeze
Blowing over the meadows brown.
And one was safe and asleep in his bed
Who at the bridge would be first to fall,
Who that day would be lying dead,
Pierced by a British musket-ball.

You know the rest. In the books you have read,
How the British Regulars fired and fled,—
How the farmers gave them ball for ball,
From behind each fence and farmyard wall,
Chasing the redcoats down the lane,
Then crossing the fields to emerge again
Under the trees at the turn of the road,
And only pausing to fire and load.

So through the night rode Paul Revere;
And so through the night went his cry of alarm
To every Middlesex village and farm,—
A cry of defiance and not of fear,
A voice in the darkness, a knock at the door,
And a word that shall echo forevermore!
For, borne on the night-wind of the Past,
Through all our history, to the last,
In the hour of darkness and peril and need,
The people will waken and listen to hear
The hurrying hoofbeats of that steed,
And the midnight message of Paul Revere.

HAWTHORNE

MAY 23, 1864

How beautiful it was, that one bright day
   In the long week of rain!
Though all its splendor could not chase away
   The omnipresent pain.

The lovely town was white with apple-blooms,
   And the great elms o'erhead
Dark shadows wove on their aërial looms
   Shot through with golden thread.

Across the meadows, by the gray old manse,
   The historic river flowed:
I was as one who wanders in a trance,
   Unconscious of his road.

The faces of familiar friends seemed strange;
   Their voices I could hear,
And yet the words they uttered seemed to change
   Their meaning to my ear.

For the one face I looked for was not there,
   The one low voice was mute;
Only an unseen presence filled the air,
   And baffled my pursuit.

Now I look back, and meadow, manse, and stream
   Dimly my thought defines;
I only see—a dream within a dream—
   The hilltop hearsed with pines.

I only hear above his place of rest
   Their tender undertone,
The infinite longings of a troubled breast,
   The voice so like his own.

There in seclusion and remote from men
   The wizard hand lies cold,
Which at its topmost speed let fall the pen,
   And left the tale half told.

Ah! who shall lift that wand of magic power,
   And the lost clue regain?
The unfinished window in Aladdin's tower
   Unfinished must remain!

AFTERMATH

When the summer fields are mown,
When the birds are fledged and flown,
   And the dry leaves strew the path;
With the falling of the snow,
With the cawing of the crow,
Once again the fields we mow
   And gather in the aftermath.

Not the sweet, new grass with flowers
Is this harvesting of ours;
   Not the upland clover bloom;
But the rowen mixed with weeds,
Tangled tufts from marsh and meads,
Where the poppy drops its seeds
   In the silence and the gloom.

NATURE

As fond mother, when the day is o'er,
    Leads by the hand her little child to bed,
    Half willing, half reluctant to be led,
    And leave his broken playthings on the floor,
Still gazing at them through the open door,
    Nor wholly reassured and comforted
    By promises of others in their stead,
    Which, though more splendid, may not please him more;

So Nature deals with us, and takes away
    Our playthings one by one, and by the hand
    Leads us to rest so gently, that we go
Scarce knowing if we wish to go or stay,
    Being too full of sleep to understand
    How far the unknown transcends the what we know.

THE CROSS OF SNOW

In the long, sleepless watches of the night,
    A gentle face—the face of one long dead—
    Looks at me from the wall, where round its head
    The night lamp casts a halo of pale light.
Here in this room she died; and soul more white
    Never through martyrdom of fire was led
    To its repose; nor can in books be read
    The legend of a life more benedight.
There is a mountain in the distant West
    That, sun-defying, in its deep ravines
    Displays a cross of snow upon its side.
Such is the cross I wear upon my breast
    These eighteen years, through all the changing scenes
    And seasons, changeless since the day she died.

THE BELLS OF SAN BLAS

What say the Bells of San Blas
To the ships that southward pass
    From the harbor of Mazatlan?
To them it is nothing more
Than the sound of surf on the shore,—
    Nothing more to master or man.

But to me, a dreamer of dreams,
To whom what is and what seems
    Are often one and the same,—
The Bells of San Blas to me
Have a strange, wild melody,
    And are something more than a name.

For bells are the voice of the church;
They have tones that touch and search
    The hearts of young and old;
One sound to all, yet each
Lends a meaning to their speech,
    And the meaning is manifold.

They are a voice of the Past,
Of an age that is fading fast,
    Of a power austere and grand;
When the flag of Spain unfurled
Its folds o'er this western world,
    And the Priest was lord of the land.

The chapel that once looked down
On the little seaport town
    Has crumbled into the dust;

And on oaken beams below
The bells swing to and fro,
      And are green with mold and rust.

"Is, then, the old faith dead,"
They say, "and in its stead
      Is some new faith proclaimed,
That we are forced to remain
Naked to sun and rain,
      Unsheltered and ashamed?

"Once in our tower aloof
We rang over wall and roof
      Our warnings and our complaints;
And round about us there
The white doves filled the air,
      Like the white souls of the saints.

"The saints! Ah, have they grown
Forgetful of their own?
      Are they asleep, or dead,
That open to the sky
Their ruined Missions lie,
      No longer tenanted?

"Oh, bring us back once more
The vanished days of yore,
      When the world with faith was filled;
Bring back the fervid zeal,
The hearts of fire and steel,
      The hands that believe and build.

"Then from our tower again
We will send over land and main

Our voices of command,
Like exiled kings who return
To their thrones, and the people learn
    That the Priest is lord of the land!"

O Bells of San Blas, in vain
Ye call back the Past again!
    The Past is deaf to your prayer;
Out of the shadows of night
The world rolls into light;
    It is daybreak everywhere.

Evangeline

A Tale of Acadie

EVANGELINE

A TALE OF ACADIE

This is the forest primeval. The murmuring pines and
    the hemlocks,
Bearded with moss, and in garments green, indistinct
    in the twilight,
Stand like Druids of eld, with voices sad and prophetic,
Stand like harpers hoar, with beards that rest on their
    bosoms.
Loud from its rocky caverns, the deep-voiced neighboring
    ocean
Speaks, and in accents disconsolate answers the wail of
    the forest.

This is the forest primeval; but where are the hearts
    that beneath it
Leaped like the roe, when he hears in the woodland
    the voice of the huntsman?
Where is the thatch-roofed village, the home of Acadian
    farmers,—
Men whose lives glided on like rivers that water the
    woodlands,
Darkened by shadows of earth, but reflecting an image
    of heaven?
Waste are those pleasant farms, and the farmers forever
    departed!
Scattered like dust and leaves, when the mighty blasts
    of October
Seize them, and whirl them aloft, and sprinkle them
    far o'er the ocean.
Naught but tradition remains of the beautiful village
    of Grand-Pré.

Ye who believe in affection that hopes, and endures,
    and is patient,
Ye who believe in the beauty and strength of woman's
    devotion,
List to the mournful tradition, still sung by the pines
    of the forest;
List to a Tale of Love in Acadie, home of the happy.

PART THE FIRST

I

In the Acadian land, on the shores of the Basin of
    Minas,
Distant, secluded, still the little village of Grand-Pré
Lay in the fruitful valley. Vast meadows stretched to
    the eastward,
Giving the village its name, and pasture to flocks without
    number.
Dikes, that the hands of farmers had raised with labor
    incessant,
Shut out the turbulent tides; but at stated seasons the
    floodgates
Opened, and welcomed the sea to wander at will o'er
    the meadows.
West and south there were fields of flax, and orchards
    and cornfields
Spreading afar and unfenced o'er the plain; and away
    to the northward
Blomidon rose, and the forests old, and aloft on the
    mountains
Sea-fogs pitched their tents, and mists from the mighty
    Atlantic
Looked on the happy valley, but ne'er from their station
    descended.

There, in the midst of its farms, reposed the Acadian
village.
Strongly built were the houses, with frames of oak and
of hemlock,
Such as the peasants of Normandy built in the reign
of the Henries.
Thatched were the roofs, with dormer windows; and
gables projecting
Over the basement below protected and shaded the
doorway.
There in the tranquil evenings of summer, when brightly
the sunset
Lighted the village street, and gilded the vanes on the
chimneys,
Matrons and maidens sat in snow-white caps and in
kirtles
Scarlet and blue and green, with distaffs spinning the
golden
Flax for the gossiping looms, whose noisy shuttles within
doors
Mingled their sounds with the whir of the wheels and
the songs of the maidens.
Solemnly down the street came the parish priest, and
the children
Paused in their play to kiss the hand he extended to
bless them.
Reverend walked he among them; and up rose matrons
and maidens,
Hailing his slow approach with words of affectionate
welcome.
Then came the laborers home from the field, and serenely
the sun sank
Down to his rest, and twilight prevailed. Anon from
the belfry
Softly the Angelus sounded, and over the roofs of the
village

Columns of pale blue smoke, like clouds of incense
    ascending,
Rose from a hundred hearths, the home of peace and
    contentment.
Thus dwelt together in love these simple Acadian farm-
    ers,—
Dwelt in the love of God and of man. Alike were
    they free from
Fear, that reigns with the tyrant, and envy, the vice
    of republics.
Neither locks had they to their doors, nor bars to their
    windows;
But their dwellings were open as day and the hearts
    of the owners;
There the richest was poor, and the poorest lived in
    abundance.

Somewhat apart from the village, and nearer the Basin
    of Minas,
Benedict Bellefontaine, the wealthiest farmer of Grand-
    Pré,
Dwelt on his goodly acres; and with him, directing
    his household,
Gentle Evangeline lived, his child, and the pride of the
    village.
Stalworth and stately in form was the man of seventy
    winters;
Hearty and hale was he, an oak that is covered with
    snowflakes;
White as the snow were his locks, and his cheeks as
    brown as the oak leaves.
Fair was she to behold, that maiden of seventeen summers.
Black were her eyes as the berry that grows on the
    thorn by the wayside,
Black, yet how softly they gleamed beneath the brown
    shade of her tresses!

Sweet was her breath as the breath of kine that feed
in the meadows.
When in the harvest heat she bore to the reapers at
noontide
Flagons of home-brewed ale, ah! fair in sooth was the
maiden.
Fairer was she when, on Sunday morn, while the bell
from its turret
Sprinkled with holy sounds the air, as the priest with
his hyssop
Sprinkles the congregation, and scatters blessings upon
them,
Down the long street she passed, with her chaplet of
beads and her missal,
Wearing her Norman cap, and her kirtle of blue, and
the earrings,
Brought in the olden time from France, and since, as
an heirloom,
Handed down from mother to child, through long
generations.
But a celestial brightness—a more ethereal beauty—
Shone on her face and encircled her form, when, after
confession,
Homeward serenely she walked with God's benediction
upon her.
When she had passed, it seemed like the ceasing of
exquisite music.

Firmly builded with rafters of oak, the house of the
farmer
Stood on the side of a hill commanding the sea; and
a shady
Sycamore grew by the door, with a woodbine wreathing
around it.
Rudely carved was the porch, with seats beneath; and
a footpath

Led through an orchard wide, and disappeared in the
    meadow.
Under the sycamore tree were hives overhung by a
    penthouse,
Such as the traveller sees in regions remote by the
    roadside,
Built o'er a box for the poor, or the blessed image
    of Mary.
Farther down, on the slope of the hill, was the well
    with its moss-grown
Bucket, fastened with iron, and near it a trough for
    the horses.
Shielding the house from storms, on the north, were
    the barns and the farmyard.
There stood the broad-wheeled wains and the antique
    ploughs and the harrows;
There were the folds for the sheep; and there, in his
    feathered seraglio,
Strutted the lordly turkey, and crowed the cock, with
    the selfsame
Voice that in ages of old had startled the penitent
    Peter.
Bursting with hay were the barns, themselves a village.
    In each one
Far o'er the gable projected a roof of thatch; and a
    staircase,
Under the sheltering eaves, led up to the odorous corn-
    loft.
There too the dove-cot stood, with its meek and innocent
    inmates
Murmuring ever of love; while above it the variant
    breezes
Numberless noisy weathercocks rattled and sang of
    mutation.

Thus, at peace with God and the world, the farmer of Grand-Pré
Lived on his sunny farm, and Evangeline governed his household.
Many a youth, as he knelt in church and opened his missal,
Fixed his eyes upon her as the saint of his deepest devotion;
Happy was he who might touch her hand or the hem of her garment!
Many a suitor came to her door, by the darkness befriended,
And, as he knocked and waited to hear the sound of her footsteps,
Knew not which beat the louder, his heart or the knocker of iron;
Or at the joyous feast of the Patron Saint of the village,
Bolder grew, and pressed her hand in the dance as he whispered
Hurried words of love, that seemed a part of the music.
But, among all who came, young Gabriel only was welcome;
Gabriel Lajeunesse, the son of Basil the blacksmith,
Who was a mighty man in the village, and honored of all men;
For, since the birth of time, throughout all ages and nations,
Has the craft of the Smith been held in repute by the people.
Basil was Benedict's friend. Their children from earliest childhood
Grew up together as brother and sister; and Father Felician,
Priest and pedagogue both in the village, had taught them their letters

Out of the selfsame book, with the hymns of the
church and the plain-song.
But when the hymn was sung, and the daily lesson
completed,
Swiftly they hurried away to the forge of Basil the
blacksmith.
There at the door they stood, with wondering eyes to
behold him
Take in his leathern lap the hoof of the horse as a
plaything,
Nailing the shoe in its place; while near him the tire
of the cartwheel
Lay like a fiery snake, coiled round in a circle of
cinders.
Oft on autumnal eves, when without in the gathering
darkness
Bursting with light seemed the smithy, through every
cranny and crevice,
Warm by the forge within they watched the laboring
bellows,
And as its panting ceased, and the sparks expired in
the ashes,
Merrily laughed, and said they were nuns going into
the chapel.
Oft on sledges in winter, as swift as the swoop of
the eagle,
Down the hillside bounding, they glided away o'er the
meadow.
Oft in the barns they climbed to the populous nests
on the rafters,
Seeking with eager eyes that wondrous stone, which
the swallow
Brings from the shore of the sea to restore the sight
of its fledglings;
Lucky was he who found that stone in the nest of
the swallow!

Thus passed a few swift years, and they no longer
    were children.
He was a valiant youth, and his face, like the face of
    the morning,
Gladdened the earth with its light, and ripened thought
    into action.
She was a woman now, with the heart and hopes of
    a woman.
"Sunshine of Saint Eulalie" was she called; for that was
    the sunshine
Which, as the farmers believed, would load their orchards
    with apples;
She, too, would bring to her husband's house delight
    and abundance,
Filling it with love and the ruddy faces of children.

II

Now had the season returned, when the nights grow
    colder and longer,
And the retreating sun the sign of the Scorpion enters.
Birds of passage sailed through the leaden air, from
    the ice-bound,
Desolate northern bays to the shores of tropical islands
Harvests were gathered in; and wild with the winds
    of September
Wrestled the trees of the forest, as Jacob of old with
    the angel.
All the signs foretold a winter long and inclement.
Bees, with prophetic instinct of want, had hoarded their
    honey
Till the hives overflowed; and the Indian hunters asserted
Cold would the winter be, for thick was the fur of
    the foxes.
Such was the advent of autumn. Then followed that
    beautiful season,

Called by the pious Acadian peasants the Summer of
    All-Saints!
Filled was the air with a dreamy and magical light;
    and the landscape
Lay as if new-created in all the freshness of childhood.
Peace seemed to reign upon the earth, and the restless
    heart of the ocean
Was for a moment consoled. All sounds were in harmony
    blended.
Voices of children at play, the crowing of cocks in
    the farmyards,
Whir of wings in the drowsy air, and the cooing of
    pigeons,
All were subdued and low as the murmurs of love,
    and the great sun
Looked with the eye of love through the golden vapors
    around him;
While arrayed in its robes of russet and scarlet and
    yellow,
Bright with the sheen of the dew, each glittering tree
    of the forest
Flashed like the plane tree the Persian adorned with
    mantles and jewels.

Now recommenced the reign of rest and affection
    and stillness.
Day with its burden and heat had departed, and twilight
    descending
Brought back the evening star to the sky, and the
    herds to the homestead.
Pawing the ground they came, and resting their necks
    on each other,
And with their nostrils distended inhaling the freshness
    of evening.
Foremost, bearing the bell, Evangeline's beautiful heifer,

Proud of her snow-white hide, and the ribbon that
 waved from her collar,
Quietly paced and slow, as if conscious of human
 affection.
Then came the shepherd back with his bleating flocks
 from the seaside,
Where was their favorite pasture. Behind them followed
 the watch-dog,
Patient, full of importance, and grand in the pride of
 his instinct,
Walking from side to side with a lordly air, and superbly
Waving his bushy tail, and urging forward the stragglers;
Regent of flocks was he when the shepherd slept; their
 protector,
When from the forest at night, through the starry silence
 the wolves howled.
Late, with the rising moon, returned the wains from
 the marshes,
Laden with briny hay, that filled the air with its odor.
Cheerily neighed the steeds, with dew on their manes
 and their fetlocks,
While aloft on their shoulders the wooden and ponderous
 saddles,
Painted with brilliant dyes, and adorned with tassels of
 crimson,
Nodded in bright array, like hollyhocks heavy with
 blossoms.
Patiently stood the cows meanwhile, and yielded their
 udders
Unto the milkmaid's hand; whilst loud and in regular
 cadence
Into the sounding pails the foaming streamlets descended.
Lowing of cattle and peals of laughter were heard in
 the farmyard,
Echoed back by the barns. Anon they sank into stillness;

Heavily closed, with a jarring sound, the valves of the
barn doors,
Rattled the wooden bars, and all for a season was silent.

Indoors, warm by the wide-mouthed fireplace, idly
the farmer
Sat in his elbow-chair and watched how the flames and
the smoke-wreaths
Struggled together like foes in a burning city. Behind
him,
Nodding and mocking along the wall, with gestures
fantastic,
Darted his own huge shadow, and vanished away into
darkness.
Faces, clumsily carved in oak, on the back of his arm-
chair
Laughed in the flickering light; and the pewter plates
on the dresser
Caught and reflected the flame, as shields of armies the
sunshine.
Fragments of song the old man sang, and carols of
Christmas,
Such as at home, in the olden time, his fathers before
him
Sang in their Norman orchards and bright Burgundian
vineyards.
Close at her father's side was the gentle Evangeline
seated,
Spinning flax for the loom, that stood in the corner
behind her,
Silent awhile were its treadles, at rest was its diligent
shuttle,
While the monotonous drone of the wheel, like the
drone of a bagpipe,
Followed the old man's song and united the fragments
together.

As in a church, when the chant of the choir at intervals
    ceases,
Footfalls are heard in the aisles, or words of the priest
    at the altar,
So, in each pause of the song, with measured motion
    the clock clicked.

Thus as they sat, there were footsteps heard, and,
    suddenly lifted,
Sounded the wooden latch, and the door swung back
    on its hinges.
Benedict knew by the hobnailed shoes it was Basil
    the blacksmith,
And by her beating heart Evangeline knew who was
    with him.
"Welcome!" the farmer exclaimed, as their footsteps
    paused on the threshold,
"Welcome, Basil, my friend! Come, take thy place on
    the settle
Close by the chimney-side, which is always empty
    without thee;
Take from the shelf overhead thy pipe and the box
    of tobacco;
Never so much thyself art thou as when through the
    curling
Smoke of the pipe or the forge thy friendly and jovial
    face gleams
Round and red as the harvest moon through the mist
    of the marshes."
Then, with a smile of content, thus answered Basil the
    blacksmith,
Taking with easy air the accustomed seat by the fireside:
"Benedict Bellefontaine, thou hast ever thy jest and thy
    ballad!
Ever in cheerfullest mood art thou, when others are
    filled with

Gloomy forebodings of ill, and see only ruin before
them.
Happy art thou, as if every day thou hadst picked up
a horseshoe."
Pausing a moment, to take the pipe that Evangeline
brought him,
And with a coal from the embers had lighted, he slowly
continued:
"Four days now are passed since the English ships at
their anchors
Ride in the Gaspereau's mouth, with their cannon pointed
against us.
What their design may be is unknown; but all are
commanded
On the morrow to meet in the church, where his
Majesty's mandate
Will be proclaimed as law in the land. Alas! in the
meantime
Many surmises of evil alarm the hearts of the people."
Then made answer the farmer: "Perhaps some friendlier
purpose
Brings these ships to our shores. Perhaps the harvests
in England
By untimely rains or untimelier heat have been blighted,
And from our bursting barns they would feed their
cattle and children."
"Not so thinketh the folk in the village," said, warmly,
the blacksmith,
Shaking his head, as in doubt; then, heaving a sigh,
he continued:
"Louisburg is not forgotten, nor Beau Séjour, nor Port
Royal.
Many already have fled to the forest, and lurk on its
outskirts,
Waiting with anxious hearts the dubious fate of to-
morrow.

Arms have been taken from us, and warlike weapons
of all kinds;
Nothing is left but the blacksmith's sledge and the
scythe of the mower."
Then with a pleasant smile made answer the jovial
farmer:
"Safer are we unarmed, in the midst of our flocks and
our cornfields,
Safer within these peaceful dikes, besieged by the ocean,
Than our fathers in forts, besieged by the enemy's
cannon.
Fear no evil, my friend, and tonight may no shadow
of sorrow
Fall on this house and hearth; for this is the night of
the contract.
Built are the house and the barn. The merry lads of
the village
Strongly have built them and well; and, breaking the
glebe round about them,
Filled the barn with hay, and the house with food for
a twelvemonth.
René Leblanc will be here anon, with his papers and
inkhorn.
Shall we not then be glad, and rejoice in the joy of
our children?"
As apart by the window she stood, with her hand in
her lover's,
Blushing Evangeline heard the words that her father
had spoken,
And, as they died on his lips, the worthy notary entered.

III

Bent like a laboring oar, that toils in the surf of the
    ocean,
Bent, but not broken, by age was the form of the
    notary public;
Shocks of yellow hair, like the silken floss of the maize,
    hung
Over his shoulders; his forehead was high; and glasses
    with horn bows
Sat astride on his nose, with a look of wisdom supernal.
Father of twenty children was he, and more than a
    hundred
Children's children rode on his knee, and heard his
    great watch tick.
Four long years in the time of the war had he languished
    a captive,
Suffering much in an old French fort as the friend of
    the English.
Now, though warier grown, without all guile or suspicion,
Ripe in wisdom was he, but patient, and simple, and
    childlike.
He was beloved by all, and most of all by the children;
For he told them tales of the Loup-garou in the forest,
And of the goblin that came in the night to water the
    horses,
And of the white Létiche, the ghost of a child who
    unchristened
Died, and was doomed to haunt unseen the chambers
    of children;
And how on Christmas Eve the oxen talked in the stable,
And how the fever was cured by a spider shut up in
    a nutshell,
And of the marvellous powers of four-leaved clover
    and horseshoes,
With whatsoever else was writ in the lore of the village.

Then up rose from his seat by the fireside Basil the
blacksmith,
Knocked from his pipe the ashes, and slowly extending
his right hand,
"Father Leblanc," he exclaimed, "thou hast heard the
talk in the village,
And, perchance, canst tell us some news of these ships
and their errand."
Then with modest demeanor made answer the notary
public,
"Gossip enough have I heard, in sooth, yet am never
the wiser;
And what their errand may be I know not better than
others.
Yet am I not of those who imagine some evil intention
Brings them here, for we are at peace; and why then
molest us?"
"God's name!" shouted the hasty and somewhat irascible
blacksmith;
"Must we in all things look for the how, and the
why, and the wherefore?
Daily injustice is done, and might is the right of the
strongest!"
But without heeding his warmth, continued the notary
public,
"Man is unjust, but God is just; and finally justice
Triumphs; and well I remember a story, that often
consoled me,
When as a captive I lay in the old French fort at Port
Royal."
This was the old man's favorite tale, and he loved to
repeat it
When his neighbors complained that any injustice was
done them.
"Once in an ancient city, whose name I no longer
remember,

Raised aloft on a column, a brazen statue of Justice
Stood in the public square, upholding the scales in its
    left hand,
And in its right a sword, as an emblem that justice
    presided
Over the laws of the land, and the hearts and homes
    of the people.
Even the birds had built their nests in the scales of
    the balance,
Having no fear of the sword that flashed in the sunshine
    above them.
But in the course of time the laws of the land were
    corrupted;
Might took the place of right, and the weak were
    oppressed, and the mighty
Ruled with an iron rod. Then it chanced in a nobleman's
    palace
That a necklace of pearls was lost, and ere long a
    suspicion
Fell on an orphan girl who lived as a maid in the
    household.
She, after form of trial condemned to die on the scaffold,
Patiently met her doom at the foot of the statue of
    Justice.
As to her Father in heaven her innocent spirit ascended,
Lo! o'er the city a tempest rose; and the bolts of the
    thunder
Smote the statue of bronze, and hurled in wrath from
    its left hand
Down on the pavement below the clattering scales of
    the balance,
And in the hollow thereof was found the nest of a
    magpie,
Into whose clay-built walls the necklace of pearls was
    inwoven."

Silenced, but not convinced, when the story was ended,
    the blacksmith
Stood like a man who fain would speak, but findeth
    no language;
All his thoughts were congealed into lines on his face,
    as the vapors
Freeze in fantastic shapes on the windowpanes in the
    winter.

Then Evangeline lighted the brazen lamp on the table,
Filled, till it overflowed, the pewter tankard with home-
    brewed
Nut-brown ale, that was famed for its strength in the
    village of Grand-Pré;
While from his pocket the notary drew his papers and
    inkhorn,
Wrote with a steady hand the date and the age of the
    parties,
Naming the dower of the bride in flocks of sheep and
    in cattle.
Orderly all things proceeded, and duly and well were
    completed,
And the great seal of the law was set like a sun on
    the margin.
Then from his leathern pouch the farmer threw on the table
Three times the old man's fee in solid pieces of silver;
And the notary rising, and blessing the bride and the
    bridegroom,
Lifted aloft the tankard of ale and drank to their welfare.
Wiping the foam from his lip, he solemnly bowed and
    departed,
While in silence the others sat and mused by the fireside,
Till Evangeline brought the draught board out of its
    corner.
Soon was the game begun. In friendly contention the
    old men

Laughed at each lucky hit, or unsuccessful manœuvre,
Laughed when a man was crowned, or a breach was
    made in the king-row.
Meanwhile apart, in the twilight gloom of a window's
    embrasure,
Sat the lovers, and whispered together, beholding the
    moon rise
Over the pallid sea, and the silvery mists of the meadows.
Silently one by one, in the infinite meadows of heaven,
Blossomed the lovely stars, the forget-me-nots of the
    angels.

That was the evening passed. Anon the bell from
    the belfry
Rang out the hour of nine, the village curfew, and
    straightaway
Rose the guests and departed; and silence reigned in
    the household.
Many a farewell word and sweet good-night on the
    doorstep
Lingered long in Evangeline's heart, and filled it with
    gladness.
Carefully then were covered the embers that glowed
    on the hearth-stone,
And on the oaken stairs resounded the tread of the
    farmer.
Soon with a soundless step the foot of Evangeline
    followed.
Up the staircase moved a luminous space in the darkness,
Lighted less by the lamp than the shining face of the
    maiden.
Silent she passed the hall, and entered the door of her
    chamber.
Simple that chamber was, with its curtains of white,
    and its clothespress

Ample and high, on whose spacious shelves were carefully
  folded
Linen and woollen stuffs by the hand of Evangeline
  woven.
This was the precious dower she would bring to her
  husband in marriage,
Better than flocks and herds, being proofs of her skill
  as a housewife.
Soon she extinguished her lamp, for the mellow and
  radiant moonlight
Streamed through the windows, and lighted the room,
  till the heart of the maiden
Swelled and obeyed its power, like the tremulous tides
  of the ocean.
Ah! she was fair, exceeding fair to behold, as she stood
  with
Naked snow-white feet on the gleaming floor of her
  chamber!
Little she dreamed that below, among the trees of the
  orchard,
Waited her lover and watched for the gleam of her
  lamp and her shadow.
Yet were her thoughts of him, and at times a feeling
  of sadness
Passed o'er her soul, as the sailing shade of clouds in
  the moonlight
Flitted across the floor and darkened the room for a
  moment.
And, as she gazed from the window, she saw serenely
  the moon pass
Forth from the folds of a cloud, and one star follow
  her footsteps,
As out of Abraham's tent young Ishmael wandered with
  Hagar!

IV

Pleasantly rose next morn the sun on the village of
Grand-Pré.

Pleasantly gleamed in the soft, sweet air the Basin of
Minas,

Where the ships, with their wavering shadows, were
riding at anchor.

Life had long been astir in the village, and clamorous
labor

Knocked with its hundred hands at the golden gates
of the morning.

Now from the country around, from the farms and
neighboring hamlets,

Came in their holiday dresses the blithe Acadian peasants.

Many a glad good-morrow and jocund laugh from the
young folk

Made the bright air brighter, as up from the numerous
meadows,

Where no path could be seen but the track of wheels
in the greensward,

Group after group appeared, and joined, or passed on
the highway.

Long ere noon, in the village all sounds of labor were
silenced.

Thronged were the streets with people; and noisy groups
at the house-doors

Sat in the cheerful sun, and rejoiced and gossiped
together.

Every house was an inn, where all were welcomed and
feasted;

For with this simple people, who lived like brothers
together,

All things were held in common, and what one had
was another's.

Yet under Benedict's roof hospitality seemed more abun-
dant:
For Evangeline stood among the guests of her father;
Bright was her face with smiles, and words of welcome
and gladness
Fell from her beautiful lips, and blessed the cup as she
gave it.

Under the open sky, in the odorous air of the orchard,
Stript of its golden fruit, was spread the feast of
betrothal.
There in the shade of the porch were the priest and
the notary seated;
There good Benedict sat, and sturdy Basil the black-
smith.
Not far withdrawn from these, by the cider press and
the beehives,
Michael the fiddler was placed, with the gayest of hearts
and of waistcoats.
Shadow and light from the leaves alternately played on
his snow-white
Hair, as it waved in the wind; and the jolly face of
the fiddler
Glowed like a living coal when the ashes are blown
from the embers.
Gayly the old man sang to the vibrant sound of his
fiddle,
Tous les Bourgeois de Chartres, and *Le Carillon de Dun-
querque,*
And anon with his wooden shoes beat time to the
music.
Merrily, merrily whirled the wheels of the dizzying
dances
Under the orchard trees and down the path to the
meadows;

Old folk and young together, and children mingled
among them.
Fairest of all the maids was Evangeline, Benedict's
daughter!
Noblest of all the youths was Gabriel, son of the
blacksmith!

So passed the morning away. And lo! with a summons
sonorous
Sounded the bell from its tower, and over the meadows
a drum beat.
Thronged ere long was the church with men. Without,
in the churchyard,
Waited the women. They stood by the graves, and
hung on the headstones
Garlands of autumn leaves and evergreens fresh from
the forest.
Then came the guard from the ships, and marching
proudly among them
Entered the sacred portal. With loud and dissonant
clangor
Echoed the sound of their brazen drums from ceiling
and casement,—
Echoed a moment only, and slowly the ponderous
portal
Closed, and in silence the crowd awaited the will of
the soldiers.
Then uprose their commander, and spake from the steps
of the altar,
Holding aloft in his hands, with its seals, the royal
commission.
"You are convened this day," he said, "by his Majesty's
orders.
Clement and kind has he been; but how you have
answered his kindness,

Let our own hearts reply! To my natural make and
my temper
Painful the task is I do, which to you I know must
be grievous.
Yet must I bow and obey, and deliver the will of our
monarch;
Namely, that all your lands, and dwellings, and cattle
of all kinds
Forfeited be to the crown; and that you yourselves
from this province
Be transported to other lands. God grant you may
dwell there
Ever as faithful subjects, a happy and peaceable people!
Prisoners now I declare you; for such is his Majesty's
pleasure!"
As, when the air is serene in sultry solstice of summer,
Suddenly gathers a storm, and the deadly sling of the
hailstones
Beats down the farmer's corn in the field and shatters
his windows,
Hiding the sun, and strewing the ground with thatch
from the house-roofs,
Bellowing fly the herds, and seek to break their enclosures;
So on the hearts of the people descended the words
of the speaker.
Silent a moment they stood in speechless wonder, and
then arose
Louder and ever louder a wail of sorrow and anger,
And, by one impulse moved, they madly rushed to
the doorway.
Vain was the hope of escape; and cries and fierce
imprecations
Rang through the house of prayer; and high o'er the
heads of the others
Rose, with his arms uplifted, the figure of Basil the
blacksmith,

As, on a stormy sea, a spar is tossed by the billows.
Flushed was his face and distorted with passion; and
wildly he shouted,
"Down with the tyrants of England! We never have
sworn them allegiance!
Death to these foreign soldiers, who seize on our homes
and our harvests!"
More he fain would have said, but the merciless hand
of a soldier
Smote him upon the mouth, and dragged him down
to the pavement.

In the midst of the strife and tumult of angry contention,
Lo! the door of the chancel opened, and Father Felician
Entered, with serious mien, and ascended the steps of
the altar.
Raising his reverend hand, with a gesture he awed into
silence
All that clamorous throng; and thus he spake to his
people;
Deep were his tones and solemn; in accents measured
and mournful
Spake he, as, after the tocsin's alarum, distinctly the
clock strikes.
"What is this that ye do, my children? what madness
has seized you?
Forty years of my life have I labored among you, and
taught you,
Not in word alone, but in deed, to love one another!
Is this the fruit of my toils, of my vigils and prayers
and privations?
Have you so soon forgotten all lessons of love and
forgiveness?
This is the house of the Prince of Peace, and would
you profane it

Thus with violent deeds and hearts overflowing with hatred?
Lo! where the crucified Christ from his cross is gazing upon you!
See! in those sorrowful eyes what meekness and holy compassion!
Hark! how those lips still repeat the prayer, 'O Father, forgive them!'
Let us repeat that prayer in the hour when the wicked assail us,
Let us repeat it now, and say, 'O Father, forgive them!' "
Few were his words of rebuke, but deep in the hearts of his people
Sank they, and sobs of contrition succeeded the passionate outbreak,
While they repeated his prayer, and said, "O Father, forgive them!"

Then came the evening service. The tapers gleamed from the altar.
Fervent and deep was the voice of the priest, and the people responded,
Not with their lips alone, but their hearts; and the Ave Maria
Sang they, and fell on their knees, and their souls, with devotion translated,
Rose on the ardor of prayer, like Elijah ascending to heaven.

Meanwhile had spread in the village the tidings of ill, and on all sides
Wandered, wailing, from house to house the women and children.
Long at her father's door Evangeline stood, with her right hand

Shielding her eyes from the level rays of the sun, that, descending,
Lighted the village street with mysterious splendor, and roofed each
Peasant's cottage with golden thatch, and emblazoned its windows.
Long within had been spread the snow-white cloth on the table;
There stood the wheaten loaf, and the honey fragrant with wild-flowers;
There stood the tankard of ale, and the cheese fresh brought from the dairy,
And, at the head of the board, the great armchair of the farmer.
Thus did Evangeline wait at her father's door, as the sunset
Threw the long shadows of trees o'er the broad ambrosial meadows.
Ah! on her spirit within a deeper shadow had fallen,
And from the fields of her soul a fragrance celestial ascended,—
Charity, meekness, love, and hope, and forgiveness, and patience!
Then, all-forgetful of self, she wandered into the village,
Cheering with looks and words the mournful hearts of the women,
As o'er the darkening fields with lingering steps they departed,
Urged by their household cares, and the weary feet of their children.
Down sank the great red sun, and in golden, glimmering vapors
Veiled the light of his face, like the Prophet descending from Sinai.
Sweetly over the village the bell of the Angelus sounded.

Meanwhile, amid the gloom, by the church Evangeline
lingered.

All was silent within; and in vain at the door and the
windows

Stood she, and listened and looked, till, overcome by
emotion,

"Gabriel!" cried she aloud with tremulous voice; but
no answer

Came from the graves of the dead, nor the gloomier
grave of the living.

Slowly at length she returned to the tenantless house
of her father.

Smouldered the fire on the hearth, on the board was
the supper untasted,

Empty and drear was each room, and haunted with
phantoms of terror.

Sadly echoed her step on the stair and the floor of
her chamber.

In the dead of the night she heard the disconsolate rain
fall

Loud on the withered leaves of the sycamore tree by
the window.

Keenly the lightning flashed; and the voice of the echoing
thunder

Told her that God was in heaven, and governed the
world he created!

Then she remembered the tale she had heard of the
justice of Heaven;

Soothed was her troubled soul, and she peacefully
slumbered till morning.

V

Four times the sun had risen and set; and now on the
    fifth day
Cheerily called the cock to the sleeping maids of the
    farmhouse.
Soon o'er the yellow fields, in silent and mournful
    procession,
Came from the neighboring hamlets and farms the
    Acadian women,
Driving in ponderous wains their household goods to
    the seashore,
Pausing and looking back to gaze once more on their
    dwellings,
Ere they were shut from sight by the winding road
    and the woodland.
Close at their sides their children ran, and urged on
    the oxen,
While in their little hands they clasped some fragments
    of playthings.

Thus to the Gaspereau's mouth they hurried; and
    there on the sea-beach
Piled in confusion lay the household goods of the
    peasants.
All day long between the shore and the ships did the
    boats ply;
All day long the wains came laboring down from the
    village.
Late in the afternoon, when the sun was near to his
    setting,
Echoed far o'er the fields came the roll of drums from
    the churchyard.
Thither the women and children thronged. On a sudden
    the church doors

Opened, and forth came the guard, and marching in
 gloomy procession
Followed the long-imprisoned, but patient, Acadian farm-
 ers.
Even as pilgrims, who journey afar from their homes
 and their country,
Sing as they go, and in singing forget they are weary
 and wayworn,
So with songs on their lips the Acadian peasants descended
Down from the church to the shore, amid their wives
 and their daughters.
Foremost the young men came; and, raising together
 their voices,
Sang with tremulous lips a chant of the Catholic Missions:
"Sacred heart of the Savior! O inexhaustible fountain!
Fill our hearts this day with strength and submission
 and patience!"
Then the old men, as they marched, and the women
 that stood by the wayside
Joined in the sacred psalm, and the birds in the sunshine
 above them
Mingled their notes therewith, like voices of spirits
 departed.

Halfway down to the shore Evangeline waited in
 silence,
Not overcome with grief, but strong in the hour of
 affliction,—
Calmly and sadly she waited, until the procession
 approached her,
And she beheld the face of Gabriel pale with emotion.
Tears then filled her eyes, and eagerly running to meet
 him,
Clasped she his hands, and laid her head on his shoulder,
 and whispered,
"Gabriel! be of good cheer! for if we love one another

Nothing, in truth, can harm us, whatever mischances
    may happen!"
Smiling she spake these words; then suddenly paused,
    for her father
Saw she slowly advancing. Alas! how changed was his
    aspect!
Gone was the glow from his cheek, and the fire from
    his eye, and his footstep
Heavier seemed with the weight of the heavy heart in
    his bosom.
But with a smile and a sigh, she clasped his neck and
    embraced him,
Speaking words of endearment where words of comfort
    availed not.
Thus to the Gaspereau's mouth moved on that mournful
    procession.

There disorder prevailed, and the tumult and stir of
    embarking.
Busily plied the freighted boats; and in the confusion
Wives were torn from their husbands, and mothers,
    too late, saw their children
Left on the land, extending their arms, with wildest
    entreaties.
So unto separate ships were Basil and Gabriel carried,
While in despair on the shore Evangeline stood with
    her father.
Half the task was not done when the sun went down,
    and the twilight
Deepened and darkened around; and in haste the refluent
    ocean
Fled away from the shore, and left the line of the
    sand-beach
Covered with waifs of the tide, with kelp and the
    slippery seaweed.

Farther back in the midst of the household goods and
the wagons,
Like to a gypsy camp, or a leaguer after a battle,
All escape cut off by the sea, and the sentinels near
them,
Lay encamped for the night the houseless Acadian farmers.
Back to its nethermost caves retreated the bellowing
ocean,
Dragging adown the beach the rattling pebbles, and
leaving
Inland and far up the shore the stranded boats of the
sailors.
Then, as the night descended, the herds returned from
their pastures;
Sweet was the moist still air with the odor of milk
from their udders;
Lowing they waited, and long, at the well-known bars
of the farmyard,—
Waited and looked in vain for the voice and the hand
of the milkmaid.
Silence reigned in the streets; from the church no Angelus
sounded,
Rose no smoke from the roofs, and gleamed no lights
from the windows.

But on the shores meanwhile the evening fires had
been kindled,
Built of the driftwood thrown on the sands from
wrecks in the tempest.
Round them shapes of gloom and sorrowful faces were
gathered,
Voices of women were heard, and of men, and the
crying of children.
Onward from fire to fire, as from hearth to hearth in
his parish,

Wandered the faithful priest, consoling and blessing and
cheering,
Like unto shipwrecked Paul on Melita's desolate sea-
shore.
Thus he approached the place where Evangeline sat with
her father,
And in the flickering light beheld the face of the old
man,
Haggard and hollow and wan, and without either thought
or emotion,
E'en as the face of a clock from which the hands have
been taken.
Vainly Evangeline strove with words and caresses to
cheer him,
Vainly offered him food; yet he moved not, he looked
not, he spake not,
But, with a vacant stare, ever gazed at the flickering
firelight.
"Benedicite!" murmured the priest, in tones of com-
passion.
More he fain would have said, but his heart was full,
and his accents
Faltered and paused on his lips, as the feet of a child
on the threshold,
Hushed by the scene he beholds, and the awful presence
of sorrow.
Silently, therefore, he laid his hand on the head of the
maiden,
Raising his tearful eyes to the silent stars that above
them
Moved on their way, unperturbed by the wrongs and
sorrows of mortals.
Then sat he down at her side, and they wept together
in silence.

Suddenly rose from the south a light, as in autumn
    the blood-red

Moon climbs the crystal walls of heaven, and o'er the
    horizon

Titan-like stretches its hundred hands upon the mountain
    and meadow,

Seizing the rocks and the rivers, and piling huge shadows
    together.

Broader and ever broader it gleamed on the roofs of
    the village,

Gleamed on the sky and sea, and the ships that lay
    in the roadstead.

Columns of shining smoke uprose, and flashes of flame
    were

Thrust through their folds and withdrawn, like the
    quivering hands of a martyr.

Then as the wind seized the gleeds and the burning
    thatch, and, uplifting,

Whirled them aloft through the air, at once from a
    hundred housetops

Started the sheeted smoke with flashes of flame inter-
    mingled.

These things beheld in dismay the crowd on the
    shore and on shipboard.

Speechless at first they stood, then cried aloud in their
    anguish,

"We shall behold no more our homes in the village
    of Grand-Pré!"

Loud on a sudden the cocks began to crow in the
    farmyards,

Thinking the day had dawned; and anon the lowing
    of cattle

Came on the evening breeze, by the barking of dogs
    interrupted.

Then rose a sound of dread, such as startles the sleeping
        encampments
Far in the Western prairies of forests that skirt the
        Nebraska,
When the wild horses affrighted sweep by with the
        speed of the whirlwind,
Or the loud bellowing herds of buffaloes rush to the
        river.
Such was the sound that arose on the night, as the
        herds and the horses
Broke through their folds and fences, and madly rushed
        o'er the meadows.

Overwhelmed with the sight, yet speechless, the priest
        and the maiden
Gazed on the scene of terror that reddened and widened
        before them;
And as they turned at length to speak to their silent
        companion,
Lo! from his seat he had fallen, and stretched abroad
        on the seashore
Motionless lay his form, from which the soul had
        departed.
Slowly the priest uplifted the lifeless head, and the
        maiden
Knelt at her father's side, and wailed aloud in her
        terror.
Then in a swoon she sank, and lay with her head on
        his bosom.
Through the long night she lay in deep, oblivious
        slumber;
And when she awoke from the trance, she beheld a
        multitude near her.
Faces of friends she beheld, that were mournfully gazing
        upon her,
Pallid, with tearful eyes, and looks of saddest compassion.

Still the blaze of the burning village illumined the
    landscape,
Reddened the sky overhead, and gleamed on the faces
    around her,
And like the day of doom it seemed to her wavering
    senses.
Then a familiar voice she heard, as it said to the people,
"Let us bury him here by the sea. When a happier
    season
Brings us again to our home from the unknown land
    of our exile,
Then shall his sacred dust be piously laid in the
    churchyard."
Such were the words of the priest. And there in haste
    by the seaside,
Having the glare of the burning village for funeral
    torches,
But without bell or book, they buried the farmer of
    Grand-Pré.
And as the voice of the priest repeated the service of
    sorrow,
Lo! with a mournful sound, like the voice of a vast
    congregation,
Solemnly answered the sea, and mingled its roar with
    the dirges.
'Twas the returning tide, that afar from the waste of
    the ocean,
With the first dawn of the day, came heaving and
    hurrying landward.
Then recommenced once more the stir and noise of
    embarking;
And with the ebb of the tide the ships sailed out of
    the harbor,
Leaving behind them the dead on the shore, and the
    village in ruins.

Many a weary year had passed since the burning of
    Grand-Pré,
When on the falling tide the freighted vessels departed,
Bearing a nation, with all its household gods, into exile,
Exile without an end, and without an example in story.
Far asunder, on separate coasts, the Acadians landed;
Scattered were they, like flakes of snow, when the wind
    from the northeast
Strikes aslant through the fogs that darken the Banks
    of Newfoundland.
Friendless, homeless, hopeless, they wandered from city
    to city,
From the cold lakes of the North to sultry Southern
    savannas,—
From the bleak shores of the sea to the land where
    the Father of Waters
Seizes the hills in his hands, and drags them down to
    the ocean,
Deep in their sands to bury the scattered bones of the
    mammoth.
Friends they sought and homes; and many, despairing,
    heartbroken,
Asked of the earth but a grave, and no longer a friend
    nor a fireside.
Written their history stands on tablets of stone in the
    churchyards.
Long among them was seen a maiden who waited and
    wandered,
Lowly and meek in spirit, and patiently suffering all
    things.
Fair was she and young: but alas! before her extended,

Dreary and vast and silent, the desert of life, with its
	pathway
Marked by the graves of those who had sorrowed and
	suffered before her,
Passions long extinguished, and hopes long dead and
	abandoned,
As the emigrant's way o'er the Western desert is marked
	by
Campfires long consumed, and bones that bleach in
	the sunshine.
Something there was in her life incomplete, imperfect,
	unfinished;
As if a morning of June, with all its music and sunshine,
Suddenly paused in the sky, and, fading, slowly descended
Into the east again, from whence it late had arisen.
Sometimes she lingered in towns, till, urged by the
	fever within her,
Urged by a restless longing, the hunger and thirst of
	the spirit,
She would commence again her endless search and
	endeavor;
Sometimes in churchyards strayed, and gazed on the
	crosses and tombstones,
Sat by some nameless grave, and thought that perhaps
	in its bosom
He was already at rest, and she longed to slumber
	beside him.
Sometimes a rumor, a hearsay, an inarticulate whisper,
Came with its airy hand to point and beckon her
	forward.
Sometimes she spake with those who had seen her
	beloved and known him,
But it was long ago, in some far-off place or forgotten.
"Gabriel Lajeunesse!" they said; "oh, yes! we have seen
	him.

He was with Basil the blacksmith, and both have gone
.to the prairies;
Coureurs-des-Bois are they, and famous hunters and
trappers."
"Gabriel Lajeunesse!" said others; "oh yes! we have seen
him.
He is a Voyageur in the lowlands of Louisiana."
Then would they say, "Dear child! why dream and
wait for him longer?
Are there not other youths as fair as Gabriel? others
Who have hearts as tender and true; and spirits as
loyal?
Here is Baptiste Leblanc, the notary's son, who has
loved thee
Many a tedious year; come, give him thy hand and
be happy!
Thou art too fair to be left to braid St. Catherine's
tresses."
Then would Evangeline answer, serenely but sadly, "I
cannot!
Whither my heart has gone, there follows my hand,
and not elsewhere.
For when the heart goes before, like a lamp, and
illumines the pathway,
Many things are made clear, that else lie hidden in
darkness."
Thereupon the priest, her friend and father-confessor,
Said, with a smile, "O daughter! thy God thus speaketh
within thee!
Talk not of wasted affection, affection never was wasted;
If it enrich not the heart of another, its waters, returning
Back to their springs, like the rain, shall fill them full
of refreshment;
That which the fountain sends forth returns again to
the fountain,

Patience; accomplish thy labor; accomplish thy work
  of affection!
Sorrow and silence are strong, and patient endurance
  is godlike.
Therefore accomplish thy labor of love, till the heart
  is made godlike,
Purified, strengthened, perfected, and rendered more
  worthy of heaven!"
Cheered by the good man's words, Evangeline labored
  and waited.
Still in her heart she heard the funeral dirge of the
  ocean,
But with its sound there was mingled a voice that
  whispered, "Despair not!"
Thus did that poor soul wander in want and cheerless
  discomfort,
Bleeding, barefooted, over the shards and thorns of
  existence.
Let me essay, O Muse! to follow the wanderer's
  footsteps;—
Not through each devious path, each changeful year of
  existence,
But as a traveller follows a streamlet's course through
  the valley:
Far from its margin at times, and seeing the gleam of
  its water
Here and there, in some open space, and at intervals
  only;
Then drawing nearer its banks, through sylvan glooms
  that conceal it,
Though he behold it not, he can hear its continuous
  murmur;
Happy, at length, if he find the spot where it reaches
  an outlet.

II

It was the month of May. Far down the Beautiful
    River,
Past the Ohio shore and past the mouth of the Wabash,
Into the golden stream of the broad and swift Mississippi,
Floated a cumbrous boat, that was rowed by Acadian
    boatmen.
It was a band of exiles: a raft, as it were, from the
    shipwrecked
Nation, scattered along the coast, now floating together,
Bound by the bonds of a common belief and a common
    misfortune;
Men and women and children, who, guided by hope
    or by hearsay,
Sought for their kith and their kin among the few-
    acred farmers
On the Acadian coast, and the prairies of fair Opelousas.
With them Evangeline went, and her guide, the Father
    Felician.
Onward o'er sunken sands, through a wilderness somber
    with forests,
Day after day they glided down the turbulent river;
Night after night, by their blazing fires, encamped on
    its borders.
Now through rushing chutes, among green islands,
    where plumelike
Cotton trees nodded their shadowy crests, they swept
    with the current,
Then emerged into broad lagoons, where silvery sandbars
Lay in the stream, and along the wimpling waves of
    their margin,
Shining with snow-white plumes, large flocks of pelicans
    waded.
Level the landscape grew, and along the shores of the
    river,

Shaded by china trees, in the midst of luxuriant gardens,
Stood the houses of planters, with Negro cabins and
dovecots.
They were approaching the region where reigns perpetual
summer,
Where through the Golden Coast, and groves of orange
and citron,
Sweeps with majestic curve the river away to the
eastward.
They, too, swerved from their course; and, entering
the Bayou of Plaquemine,
Soon were lost in a maze of sluggish and devious
waters,
Which, like a network of steel, extended in every
direction.
Over their heads the towering and tenebrous boughs
of the cypress
Met in a dusky arch, and trailing mosses in midair
Waved like banners that hang on the walls of ancient
cathedrals.
Deathlike the silence seemed, and unbroken, save by
the herons
Home to their roosts in the cedar trees returning at
sunset,
Or by the owl, as he greeted the moon with demoniac
laughter.
Lovely the moonlight was as it glanced and gleamed
on the water,
Gleamed on the columns of cypress and cedar sustaining
the arches,
Down through whose broken vaults it fell as through
chinks in a ruin.
Dreamlike, and indistinct, and strange were all things
around them;
And o'er their spirits there came a feeling of wonder
and sadness,—

Strange forebodings of ill, unseen and that cannot be
    compassed.
As, at the tramp of a horse's hoof on the turf of the
    prairies,
Far in advance are closed the leaves of the shrinking
    mimosa,
So, at the hoofbeats of fate, with sad forebodings of
    evil,
Shrinks and closes the heart, ere the stroke of doom
    had attained it.
But Evangeline's heart was sustained by a vision, that
    faintly
Floated before her eyes, and beckoned her on through
    the moonlight.
It was the thought of her brain that assumed the shape
    of a phantom.
Through those shadowy aisles had Gabriel wandered
    before her,
And every stroke of the oar now brought him nearer
    and nearer.

Then in his place, at the prow of the boat, rose
    one of the oarsmen,
And, as a signal sound, if others like them peradventure
Sailed on those gloomy and midnight streams, blew a
    blast on his bugle.
Wild through the dark colonnades and corridors leafy
    the blast rang,
Breaking the seal of silence, and giving tongues to the
    forest.
Soundless above them the banners of moss just stirred
    to the music.
Multitudinous echoes awoke and died in the distance,
Over the watery floor, and beneath the reverberant
    branches;

But not a voice replied; no answer came from the
    darkness;
And, when the echoes had ceased, like a sense of pain
    was the silence.
Then Evangeline slept; but the boatmen rowed through
    the midnight,
Silent at times, then singing familiar Canadian boatsongs,
Such as they sang of old on their own Acadian rivers,
While through the night were heard the mysterious
    sounds of the desert,
Far off,—indistinct,—as of wave or wind in the forest,
Mixed with the whoop of the crane and the roar of
    the grim alligator.

Thus ere another noon they emerged from the shades;
    and before them
Lay, in the golden sun, the lakes of the Atchafalaya.
Water lilies in myriads rocked on the slight undulations
Made by the passing oars, and, resplendent in beauty,
    the lotus
Lifted her golden crown above the heads of the boatmen.
Faint was the air with the odorous breath of magnolia
    blossoms,
And with the heat of noon; and numberless sylvan
    islands,
Fragrant and thickly embowered with blossoming hedges
    of roses,
Near to whose shores they glided along, invited to
    slumber.
Soon by the fairest of these their weary oars were
    suspended.
Under the boughs of Wachita willows, that grew by
    the margin,
Safely their boat was moored; and scattered about on
    the greensward,

Tired with their midnight toil, the weary travellers
slumbered.
Over them vast and high extended the cope of a cedar.
Swinging from its great arms, the trumpet flower and
the grapevine
Hung their ladder of ropes aloft like the ladder of
Jacob,
On whose pendulous stairs the angels ascending, de-
scending,
Were the swift humming-birds, that flitted from blossom
to blossom.
Such was the vision Evangeline saw as she slumbered
beneath it.
Filled was her heart with love, and the dawn of an
opening heaven
Lighted her soul in sleep with the glory of regions
celestial.

Nearer, and ever nearer, among the numberless islands,
Darted a light, swift boat, that sped away o'er the
water,
Urged on its course by the sinewy arms of hunters
and trappers.
Northward its prow was turned, to the land of the
bison and beaver.
At the helm sat a youth, with countenance thoughtful
and careworn.
Dark and neglected locks overshadowed his brow, and
a sadness
Somewhat beyond his years on his face was legibly
written.
Gabriel was it, who, weary with waiting, unhappy and
restless,
Sought in the Western wilds oblivion of self and of
sorrow.

Swiftly they glided along, close under the lee of the
island,
But by the opposite bank, and behind a screen of
palmettos,
So they saw not the boat, where it lay concealed in
the willows;
All undisturbed by the dash of their oars, and unseen,
were the sleepers.
Angel of God was there none to awaken the slumbering
maiden.
Swiftly they glided away, like the shade of a cloud
on the prairie.
After the sound of their oars on the tholes had died
in the distance,
As from a magic trance the sleepers awoke, and the
maiden
Said with a sigh to the friendly priest, "O Father
Felician!
Something says in my heart that near me Gabriel wanders.
Is it a foolish dream, an idle and vague superstition?
Or has an angel passed, and revealed the truth to my
spirit?"
Then, with a blush, she added, "Alas for my credulous
fancy!
Unto ears like thine such words as these have no
meaning."
But made answer the reverend man, and he smiled as
he answered,
"Daughter, thy words are not idle; nor are they to
me without meaning.
Feeling is deep and still; and the word that floats on
the surface
Is as the tossing buoy, that betrays where the anchor
is hidden.
Therefore trust to thy heart, and to what the world
calls illusions.

Gabriel truly is near thee; for not far away to the
southward
On the banks of the Têche, are the towns of St. Maur
and St. Martin.
There the long-wandering bride shall be given again
to her bridegroom,
There the long-absent pastor regain his flock and his
sheepfold.
Beautiful is the land, with its prairies and forests of
fruit trees;
Under the feet a garden of flowers, and the bluest of
heavens
Bending above, and resting its dome on the walls of
the forest.
They who dwell there have named it the Eden of
Louisiana!"

With these words of cheer they arose and continued
their journey.
Softly the evening came. The sun from the western
horizon
Like a magician extended his golden wand o'er the
landscape;
Twinkling vapor arose; and sky and water and forest
Seemed all on fire at the touch, and melted and mingled
together.
Hanging between two skies, a cloud with edges of
silver,
Floated the boat, with its dripping oars, on the motionless
water.
Filled was Evangeline's heart with inexpressible sweet-
ness.
Touched by the magic spell, the sacred fountains of
feeling
Glowed with the light of love, as the skies and waters
around her.

Then from a neighboring thicket the mockingbird,
  wildest of singers,
Swinging aloft on a willow spray that hung o'er the
  water,
Shook from his little throat such floods of delirious music,
That the whole air and the woods and the waves seemed
  silent to listen.
Plaintive at first were the tones and sad; then soaring
  to madness
Seemed they to follow or guide the revel of frenzied
  Bacchantes.
Single notes were then heard, in sorrowful, low lam-
  entation;
Till, having gathered them all, he flung them abroad
  in derision,
As when, after a storm, a gust of wind through the
  treetops
Shakes down the rattling rain in a crystal shower on
  the branches.
With such a prelude as this, and hearts that throbbed
  with emotion,
Slowly they entered the Têche, where it flows through
  the green Opelousas,
And, through the amber air, above the crest of the
  woodland,
Saw the column of smoke that rose from a neighboring
  dwelling;—
Sounds of a horn they heard, and the distant lowing
  of cattle.

III

Near to the bank of the river, o'ershadowed by oaks,
  from whose branches
Garlands of Spanish moss and of mystic mistletoe flaunted,
Such as the Druids cut down with golden hatchets at
  Yuletide,

Stood, secluded and still, the house of the herdsman.
　　　A garden
Girded it round about with a belt of luxuriant blossoms,
Filling the air with fragrance. The house itself was of
　　　timbers.
Hewn from the cypress tree, and carefully fitted together.
Large and low was the roof; and on slender columns
　　　supported,
Rose-wreathed, vine-encircled, a broad and spacious
　　　veranda,
Haunt of the hummingbird and the bee, extended
　　　around it.
At each end of the house, amid the flowers of the
　　　garden,
Stationed the dovecots were, as love's perpetual symbol,
Scenes of endless wooing, and endless contentions of
　　　rivals,
Silence reigned o'er the place. The line of shadow and
　　　sunshine
Ran near the tops of the trees; but the house itself
　　　was in shadow,
And from its chimney top, ascending and slowly ex-
　　　panding
Into the evening air, a thin blue column of smoke
　　　rose.
In the rear of the house, from the garden gate, ran
　　　a pathway
Through the great groves of oak to the skirts of the
　　　limitless prairie,
Into whose sea of flowers the sun was slowly descending.
Full in his track of light, like ships with shadowy
　　　canvas
Hanging loose from their spars in a motionless calm
　　　in the tropics,
Stood a cluster of trees, with tangled cordage of grape-
　　　vines.

Just where the woodlands met the flowery surf of
     the prairie,
Mounted upon his horse, with Spanish saddle and stirrups,
Sat a herdsman, arrayed in gaiters and doublet of deerskin.
Broad and brown was the face that from under the
     Spanish sombrero
Gazed on the peaceful scene, with the lordly look of
     its master.
Round about him were numberless herds of kine, that
     were grazing
Quietly in the meadows, and breathing the vapory
     freshness
That uprose from the river, and spread itself over the
     landscape.
Slowly lifting the horn that hung at his side, and
     expanding
Fully his broad, deep chest, he blew a blast, that
     resounded
Wildly and sweet and far, through the still damp air
     of the evening.
Suddenly out of the grass the long white horns of the
     cattle
Rose like flakes of foam on the adverse currents of
     ocean.
Silent a moment they gazed, then bellowing rushed o'er
     the prairie,
And the whole mass became a cloud, a shade in the
     distance.
Then, as the herdsman turned to the house, through
     the gate of the garden
Saw he the forms of the priest and the maiden advancing
     to meet him.
Suddenly down from his horse he sprang in amazement,
     and forward
Rushed with extended arms and exclamations of wonder;

When they beheld his face, they recognized Basil the
    blacksmith.
Hearty his welcome was, as he led his guests to the
    garden.
There in an arbor of roses with endless question and
    answer
Gave they vent to their hearts, and renewed their friendly
    embraces,
Laughing and weeping by turns, or sitting silent and
    thoughtful.
Thoughtful, for Gabriel came not; and now dark doubts
    and misgivings
Stole o'er the maiden's heart; and Basil, somewhat
    embarrassed,
Broke the silence and said, "If you came by the
    Atchafalaya,
How have you nowhere encountered my Gabriel's boat
    on the bayous?"
Over Evangeline's face at the words of Basil a shade
    passed.
Tears came into her eyes, and she said, with a tremulous
    accent,
"Gone? Is Gabriel gone?" and, concealing her face on
    his shoulder,
All her o'erburdened heart gave way, and she wept
    and lamented.
Then the good Basil said,—and his voice grew blithe
    as he said it,—
"Be of good cheer, my child; it is only today he
    departed.
Foolish boy! he has left me alone with my herds and
    my horses.
Moody and restless grown, and tried and troubled, his
    spirit
Could no longer endure the calm of this quiet existence.
Thinking ever of thee, uncertain and sorrowful ever,

Ever silent, or speaking only of thee and his troubles,
He at length had become so tedious to men and to
maidens,
Tedious even to me, that at length I bethought me,
and sent him
Unto the town of Adayes to trade for mules with the
Spaniards.
Thence he will follow the Indian trails to the Ozark
Mountains,
Hunting for furs in the forests, on rivers trapping the
beaver.
Therefore be of good cheer; we will follow the fugitive
lover;
He is not far on his way, and the Fates and the streams
are against him.
Up and away tomorrow, and through the red dew
of the morning
We will follow him fast, and bring him back to his
prison."

Then glad voices were heard, and up from the banks
of the river,
Borne aloft on his comrades' arms, came Michael the
fiddler.
Long under Basil's roof had he lived like a god on
Olympus,
Having no other care than dispensing music to mortals.
Far renowned was he for his silver locks and his fiddle.
"Long live Michael," they cried, "our brave Arcadian
minstrel!"
As they bore him aloft in triumphal procession; and
straightway
Father Felician advanced with Evangeline, greeting the
old man
Kindly and oft, and recalling the past, while Basil,
enraptured,

Hailed with hilarious joy his old companions and gossips,
Laughing loud and long, and embracing mothers and
daughters.
Much they marvelled to see the wealth of the cidevant
blacksmith,
All his domains and his herds, and his patriarchal
demeanor;
Much they marvelled to hear his tales of the soil and
the climate,
And of the prairies, whose numberless herds were his
who would take them;
Each one thought in his heart, that he, too, would go
and do likewise.
Thus they ascended the steps, and crossing the breezy
veranda,
Entered the hall of the house, where already the supper
of Basil
Waited his late return; and they rested and feasted
together.

Over the joyous feast the sudden darkness descended.
All was silent without, and, illuming the landscape with
silver,
Fair rose the dewy moon and the myriad stars; but
within doors,
Brighter than these, shone the faces of friends in the
glimmering lamplight.
Then from his station aloft, at the head of the table,
the herdsman
Poured forth his heart and his wine together in endless
profusion.
Lighting his pipe, that was filled with sweet Natchitoches
tobacco,
Thus he spake to his guests, who listened, and smiled
as they listened:

"Welcome once more, my friends, who long have been
      friendless and homeless,
Welcome once more to a home, that is better perchance
      than the old one!
Here no hungry winter congeals our blood like the
      rivers;
Here no stony ground provokes the wrath of the
      farmer.
Smoothly the ploughshare runs through the soil, as a
      keel through the water.
All the year round the orange groves are in blossom;
      and grass grows
More in a single night than a whole Canadian summer.
Here, too, numberless herds run wild and unclaimed
      in the prairies;
Here, too, lands may be had for the asking, and forests
      of timber
With a few blows of the axe are hewn and framed
      into houses.
After your houses are built, and your fields are yellow—
      with harvests,
No King George of England shall drive you away from
      your homesteads,
Burning your dwellings and barns, and stealing your
      farms and your cattle."
Speaking these words, he blew a wrathful cloud from
      his nostrils,
While his huge, brown hand came thundering down
      on the table,
So that the guests all started; and Father Felician,
      astounded,
Suddenly paused, with a pinch of snuff halfway to his
      nostrils.
But the brave Basil resumed, and his words were milder
      and gayer:

"Only beware of the fever, my friends, beware of the
      fever!
For it is not like that of our cold Acadian climate,
Cured by wearing a spider hung round one's neck in
      a nutshell!"
Then there were voices heard at the door, and footsteps
      approaching
Sounded upon the stairs and the floor of the breezy
      veranda,
It was the neighboring Creoles and small Acadian
      planters,
Who had been summoned all to the house of Basil
      the herdsman.
Merry the meeting was of ancient comrades and neigh-
      bors:
Friend clasped friend in his arms; and they who before
      were as strangers,
Meeting in exile, became straightway as friends to each
      other,
Drawn by the gentle bond of a common country together.
But in the neighboring hall a strain of music, proceeding
From the accordant strings of Michael's melodious fiddle,
Broke up all further speech. Away, like children delighted,
All things forgotten beside, they gave themselves to
      the maddening
Whirl of the giddy dance, as it swept and swayed to
      the music,
Dreamlike, with beaming eyes and the rush of fluttering
      garments.

Meanwhile, apart at the head of the hall, the priest
      and the herdsman
Sat, conversing together of past and present and future;
While Evangeline stood like one entranced, for within her
Olden memories rose, and loud in the midst of the
      music

Heard she the sound of the sea, and an irrepressible
      sadness
Came o'er her heart, and unseen she stole forth into
      the garden.
Beautiful was the night. Behind the black wall of the
      forest,
Tipping its summit with silver, arose the moon. On
      the river
Fell here and there through the branches a tremulous
      gleam of the moonlight,
Like the sweet thoughts of love on a darkened and
      devious spirit.
Nearer and round about her, the manifold flowers of
      the garden
Poured out their souls in odors, that were their prayers
      and confessions
Unto the night, as it went its way, like a silent
      Carthusian.
Fuller of fragrance than they, and as heavy with shadows
      and night-dews,
Hung the heart of the maiden. The calm and the magical
      moonlight
Seemed to inundate her soul with indefinable longings,
As, through the garden gate, and beneath the shade
      of the oak-trees,
Passed she along the path to the edge of the measureless
      prairie.
Silent it lay, with a silvery haze upon it, and fireflies
Gleamed and floated away in mingled and infinite
      numbers.
Over her head the stars, the thoughts of God in the
      heavens,
Shone on the eyes of man, who had ceased to marvel
      and worship,
Save when a blazing comet was seen on the walls of
      that temple,

As if a hand had appeared and written upon them,
    "Upharsin."
And the soul of the maiden, between the stars and the
    fireflies,
Wandered alone, and she cried, "O Gabriel! O my
    beloved!
Art thou so near unto me, and yet I cannot behold
    thee?
Art thou so near unto me, and yet thy voice does not
    reach me?
Ah! how often thy feet have trod this path to the
    prairie!
Ah! how often thine eyes have looked on the woodlands
    around me!
Ah! how often beneath this oak, returning from labor,
Thou hast lain down to rest, and to dream of me in
    thy slumbers!
When shall these eyes behold, these arms be folded
    about thee?"
Loud and sudden and near the notes of a whippoorwill
    sounded
Like a flute in the woods; and anon, through the
    neighboring thickets,
Farther and farther away it floated and dropped into
    silence.
"Patience!" whispered the oaks from oracular caverns
    of darkness:
And, from the moonlit meadow, a sigh responded, "To-
    morrow!"

Bright rose the sun next day; and all the flowers of
    the garden
Bathed his shining feet with their tears, and anointed
    his tresses
With the delicious balm that they bore in their vases
    of crystal.

"Farewell!" said the priest, as he stood at the shadowy
      threshold;
"See that you bring us the Prodigal Son from his
      fasting and famine,
And, too, the Foolish Virgin, who slept when the
      bridegroom was coming."
"Farewell!" answered the maiden, and, smiling, with
      Basil descended
Down to the river's brink, where the boatmen already
      were waiting.
Thus beginning their journey with morning, and sunshine,
      and gladness,
Swiftly they followed the flight of him who was speeding
      before them,
Blown by the blast of fate like a dead leaf over the
      desert.
Not that day, nor the next, nor yet the day that
      succeeded,
Found they the trace of his course, in lake or forest
      or river,
Nor, after many days, had they found him; but vague
      and uncertain
Rumors alone were their guides through a wild and
      desolate country;
Till, at the little inn of the Spanish town of Adayes,
Weary and worn, they alighted, and learned from the
      garrulous landlord,
That on the day before, with horses and guides and
      companions,
Gabriel left the village, and took the road of the
      prairies.

IV

Far in the West there lies a desert land, where the
    mountains
Lift, through perpetual snows, their lofty and luminous
    summits.
Down from their jagged, deep ravines, where the gorge,
    like a gateway,
Opens a passage rude to the wheels of the emigrant's
    wagon,
Westward the Oregon flows and the Walleway and
    Owyhee.
Eastward, with devious course, among the Windriver
    Mountains,
Through the Sweetwater Valley precipitate leaps the
    Nebraska;
And to the south, from Fontaine-qui-bout and the Spanish
    sierras,
Fretted with sands and rocks, and swept by the wind
    of the desert,
Numberless torrents, with ceaseless sound, descend to
    the ocean,
Like the great chords of a harp, in loud and solemn
    vibrations.
Spreading between these streams are the wondrous,
    beautiful prairies;
Billowy bays of grass ever rolling in shadow and sunshine,
Bright with luxuriant clusters of roses and purple amor-
    phas.
Over them wandered the buffalo herds, and the elk
    and the roebuck,
Over them wandered the wolves, and herds of riderless
    horses;
Fires that blast and blight, and winds that are weary
    with travel;

Over them wander the scattered tribes of Ishmael's
  children,
Staining the desert with blood; and above their terrible
  war-trails
Circles and sails aloft, on pinions majestic, the vulture,
Like the implacable soul of a chieftain slaughtered in
  battle,
By invisible stairs ascending and scaling the heavens.
Here and there rise smokes from the camps of these
  savage marauders;
Here and there rise groves from the margins of swift-
  running rivers;
And the grim, taciturn bear, the anchorite monk of
  the desert,
Climbs down their dark ravines to dig for roots by
  the brookside,
And over all is the sky, the clear and crystalline heaven,
Like the protecting hand of God inverted above them.

Into this wonderful land, at the base of the Ozark
  Mountains,
Gabriel far had entered, with hunters and trappers behind
  him.
Day after day, with their Indian guides, the maiden
  and Basil
Followed his flying steps, and thought each day to
  o'ertake him.
Sometimes they saw, or thought they saw, the smoke
  of his campfire
Rise in the morning air from the distant plain; but at
  nightfall,
When they had reached the place, they found only
  embers and ashes.
And, though their hearts were sad at times and their
  bodies were weary,
Hope still guided them on, as the magic Fata Morgana

Showed them her lakes of light, that retreated and
vanished before them.

Once, as they sat by their evening fire, there silently
entered
Into their little camp an Indian woman, whose features
Wore deep traces of sorrow, and patience as great as
her sorrow.
She was a Shawnee woman returning home to her
people,
From the far-off hunting grounds of the cruel Comanches,
Where her Canadian husband, a Coureur-des-Bois, had
been murdered.
Touched were their hearts at her story, and warmest
and friendliest welcome
Gave they, with words of cheer, and she sat and feasted
among them
On the buffalo meat and the venison cooked on the
embers.
But when their meal was done, and Basil and all his
companions,
Worn with the long day's march and the chase of the
deer and the bison,
Stretched themselves on the ground, and slept where
the quivering firelight
Flashed on their swarthy cheeks, and their forms wrapped
up in their blankets,
Then at the door of Evangeline's tent she sat and
repeated
Slowly, with soft, low voice, and the charm of her
Indian accent,
All the tale of her love, with its pleasures, and pains,
and reverses.
Much Evangeline wept at the tale, and to know that
another

Hapless heart like her own had loved and had been
    disappointed.
Moved to the depths of her soul by pity and woman's
    compassion,
Yet in her sorrow pleased that one who had suffered
    was near her,
She in turn related her love and all its disasters.
Mute with wonder the Shawnee sat, and when she had
    ended
Still was mute; but at length, as if a mysterious horror
Passed through her brain, she spake, and repeated the
    tale of the Mowis;
Mowis, the bridegroom of snow, who won and wedded
    a maiden,
But, when the morning came, arose and passed from
    the wigwam,
Fading and melting away and dissolving into the sunshine,
Till she beheld him no more, though she followed far
    into the forest.
Then, in those sweet, low tones, that seemed like a
    weird incantation,
Told she the tale of the fair Lilinau, who was wooed
    by a phantom,
That through the pines o'er her father's lodge, in the
    hush of the twilight,
Breathed like the evening wind, and whispered love to
    the maiden,
Till she followed his green and waving plume through
    the forest,
And nevermore returned, nor was seen again by her
    people.
Silent with wonder and strange surprise, Evangeline
    listened
To the soft flow of her magical words, till the region
    around her

Seemed like enchanted ground, and her swarthy guest
the enchantress.
Slowly over the tops of the Ozark Mountains the moon
rose,
Lighting the little tent, and with a mysterious splendor
Touching the somber leaves, and embracing and filling
the woodland.
With a delicious sound the brook rushed by, and the
branches
Swayed and sighed overhead in scarcely audible whispers.
Filled with the thoughts of love was Evangeline's heart,
but a secret,
Subtile sense crept in of pain and indefinite terror,
As the cold, poisonous snake creeps into the nest of
the swallow.
It was no earthly fear. A breath from the region of
spirits
Seemed to float in the air of night; and she felt for
a moment
That, like the Indian maid, she, too, was pursuing a
phantom.
With this thought she slept, and the fear and the phantom
had vanished.

Early upon the morrow the march was resumed; and
the Shawnee
Said, as they journeyed along, "On the western slope
of these mountains
Dwells in his little village the Black Robe chief of the
Mission.
Much he teaches the people, and tells them of Mary
and Jesus.
Loud laugh their hearts with joy, and weep with pain,
as they hear him."
Then, with a sudden and secret emotion, Evangeline
answered,

"Let us go to the Mission, for there good tidings await
    us!"
Thither they turned their steeds; and behind a spur of
    the mountains,
Just as the sound went down, they heard a murmur
    of voices,
And in a meadow green and broad, by the bank of
    a river,
Saw the tents of the Christians, the tents of the Jesuit
    Mission.
Under a towering oak, that stood in the midst of the
    village,
Knelt the Black Robe chief with his children. A crucifix
    fastened
High on the trunk of the tree, and overshadowed by
    grapevines,
Looked with its agonized face on the multitude kneeling
    beneath it.
This was their rural chapel. Aloft, through the intricate
    arches
Of its aerial roof, arose the chant of their vespers,
Mingling its notes with soft susurrus and sighs of the
    branches.
Silent, with heads uncovered, the travellers, nearer ap-
    proaching,
Knelt on the swarded floor, and joined in the evening
    devotions.
But when the service was done, and the benediction
    had fallen
Forth from the hands of the priest, like seed from the
    hands of the sower,
Slowly the reverend man advanced to the strangers,
    and bade them
Welcome; and when they replied, he smiled with be-
    nignant expression,

Hearing the homelike sounds of his mother tongue in
the forest,
And, with words of kindness, conducted them into his
wigwam.
There upon mats and skins they reposed, and on cakes
of the maize-ear
Feasted, and slaked their thirst from the water-gourd
of the teacher.
Soon was their story told; and the priest with solemnity
answered:
"Not six suns have risen and set since Gabriel, seated
On this mat by my side, where now the maiden reposes,
Told me this same sad tale; then arose and continued
his journey!"
Soft was the voice of the priest, and he spake with
an accent of kindness;
But on Evangeline's heart fell his words as in winter
the snowflakes
Fall into some lone nest from which the birds have
departed.
"Far to the north he has gone," continued the priest;
"but in autumn,
When the chase is done, will return again to the
Mission."
Then Evangeline said, and her voice was meek and
submissive,
"Let me remain with thee, for my soul is sad and
afflicted."
So seemed it wise and well unto all; and betimes on
the morrow,
Mounting his Mexican steed, with his Indian guides
and companions,
Homeward Basil returned, and Evangeline stayed at the
Mission.
Slowly, slowly, slowly the days succeeded each other,—

Days and weeks and months; and the fields of maize
    that were springing
Green from the ground when a stranger she came, now
    waving above her,
Lifted their slender shafts, with leaves interlacing, and
    forming
Cloisters for mendicant crows and granaries pillaged by
    squirrels.
Then in the golden weather the maize was husked, and
    the maidens
Blushed at each blood-red ear, for that betokened a
    lover,
But at the crooked laughed, and called it a thief in
    the cornfield.
Even the blood-red ear to Evangeline brought not her
    lover.
"Patience!" the priest would say; "have faith, and thy
    prayer will be answered!
Look at this vigorous plant that lifts its head from the
    meadow,
See how its leaves are turned to the north, as true as
    the magnet;
This is the compass-flower, that the finger of God has
    planted
Here in the houseless wild, to direct the traveller's
    journey
Over the sea-like, pathless, limitless waste of the desert.
Such in the soul of man is faith. The blossoms of
    passion,
Gay and luxuriant flowers, are brighter and fuller of
    fragrance,
But they beguile us, and lead us astray, and their odor
    is deadly.
Only this humble plant can guide us here, and hereafter
Crown us with asphodel flowers, that are wet with
    the dews of nepenthe."

So came the autumn, and passed, and the winter,—
    yet Gabriel came not;
Blossomed the opening spring, and the notes of the
    robin and bluebird
Sounded sweet upon wold and in wood, yet Gabriel
    came not.
But on the breath of the summer winds a rumor was
    wafted,
Sweeter than song of bird, or hue or odor of blossom.
Far to the north and east, it said, in the Michigan
    forests,
Gabriel had his lodge by the banks of the Saginaw
    River.
And, with returning guides, that sought the lakes of
    St. Lawrence,
Saying a sad farewell, Evangeline went from the Mission.
When over weary ways, by long and perilous marches,
She had attained at length the depths of the Michigan
    forests,
Found she the hunter's lodge deserted and fallen to
    ruin!

Thus did the long sad years glide on, and in seasons
    and places
Divers and distant far was seen the wandering maiden;—
Now in the Tents of Grace of the meek Moravian
    Missions,
Now in the noisy camps and the battlefields of the
    army,
Now in secluded hamlets, in towns and populous cities.
Like a phantom she came, and passed away unremem-
    bered.
Fair was she and young, when in hope began the long
    journey;
Faded was she and old, when in disappointment it
    ended.

Each succeeding year stole something away from her
    beauty,
Leaving behind it, broader and deeper, the gloom and
    the shadow.
Then there appeared and spread faint streaks of gray
    o'er her forehead,
Dawn of another life, that broke o'er her earthly horizon,
As in the eastern sky the first faint streaks of the
    morning.

V

In that delightful land which is washed by the Delaware's
    waters,
Guarding in sylvan shades the name of Penn the apostle,
Stands on the banks of its beautiful stream the city he
    founded.
There all the air is balm, and the peach is the emblem
    of beauty,
And the streets still re-ëcho the names of the trees of
    the forest,
As if they fain would appease the Dryads whose haunts
    they molested.
There from the troubled sea had Evangeline landed, an
    exile,
Finding among the children of Penn a home and a
    country.
There old René Leblanc had died; and when he departed,
Saw at his side only one of all his hundred descendants.
Something at least there was in the friendly streets of
    the city,
Something that spake to her heart, and made her no
    longer a stranger;
And her ear was pleased with the Thee and Thou of
    the Quakers,
For it recalled the past, the old Acadian country,

Where all men were equal, and all were brothers and
    sisters.
So, when the fruitless search, the disappointed endeavor,
Ended, to recommence no more upon earth, uncom-
    plaining,
Thither, as leaves to the light, were turned her thoughts
    and her footsteps.
As from the mountain's top the rainy mists of the
    morning
Roll away, and afar we behold the landscape below
    us,
Sun-illumined, with shining rivers and cities and hamlets,
So fell the mists from her mind, and she saw the
    world far below her,
Dark no longer, but all illumined with love; and the
    pathway
Which she had climbed so far, lying smooth and fair
    in the distance.
Gabriel was not forgotten. Within her heart was his
    image,
Clothed in the beauty of love and youth, at last she
    beheld him,
Only more beautiful made by this death-like silence and
    absence.
Into her thoughts of him time entered not, for it was
    not.
Over him years had no power; he was not changed,
    but transfigured;
He had become to her heart as one who is dead, and
    not absent;
Patience and abnegation of self, and devotion to others,
This was the lesson a life of trial and sorrow had
    taught her.
So was her love diffused, but, like to some odorous
    spices,

Suffered no waste nor loss, though filling the air with
    aroma.
Other hope had she none, nor wish in life, but to
    follow
Meekly, with reverent steps, the sacred feet of her
    Saviour.
Thus many years she lived as a Sister of Mercy;
    frequenting
Lonely and wretched roofs in the crowded lanes of the
    city,
Where distress and want concealed themselves from the
    sunlight,
Where disease and sorrow in garrets languished neglected.
Night after night, when the world was asleep, as the
    watchman repeated
Loud, through the gusty streets, that all was well in
    the city,
High at some lonely window he saw the light of her
    taper.
Day after day, in the gray of the dawn, as slow through
    the suburbs
Plodded the German farmer, with flowers and fruits
    for the market,
Met he that meek, pale face, returning home from its
    watchings.

Then it came to pass that a pestilence fell on the
    city,
Presaged by wonderous signs, and mostly by flocks of
    wild pigeons,
Darkening the sun in their flight, with naught in their
    craws but an acorn.
And, as the tides of the sea arise in the month of
    September,
Flooding some silver stream, till it spreads to a lake
    in the meadow,

So death flooded life, and, o'erflowing its natural margin,
Spread to a brackish lake the silver stream of existence.
Wealth had no power to bribe, nor beauty to charm,
 the oppressor;
But all perished alike beneath the scourge of his anger;—
Only, alas! the poor, who had neither friends nor
 attendants,
Crept away to die in the almshouse, home of the
 homeless.
Then in the suburbs it stood, in the midst of meadows
 and woodlands;—
Now the city surrounds it; but still, with its gateway
 and wicket
Meek, in the midst of splendor, its humble walls seem
 to echo
Softly the words of the Lord: "The poor ye always
 have with you."
Thither, by night and by day, came the Sister of Mercy.
 The dying,
Looked up into her face, and thought, indeed, to behold
 there
Gleams of celestial light encircle her forehead with
 splendor,
Such as the artist paints o'er the brows of the saints
 and apostles,
Or such as hangs by night o'er a city seen at a distance.
Unto their eyes it seemed the lamps of the city celestial,
Into whose shining gates ere long their spirits would
 enter.

Thus, on a Sabbath morn, through the streets, deserted
 and silent,
Wending her quiet way, she entered the door of the
 almshouse.
Sweet on the summer air was the odor of flowers in
 the garden;

And she paused on her way to gather the fairest among
    them,
That the dying once more might rejoice in their fragrance
    and beauty.
Then, as she mounted the stairs to the corridors, cooled
    by the east wind,
Distant and soft on her ear fell the chimes from the
    belfry of Christ Church,
While, intermingled with these, across the meadows
    were wafted
Sounds of psalms, that were sung by the Swedes in
    their church at Wicaco.
Soft as descending wings fell the calm of the hour on
    her spirit:
Something within her said, "At length thy trials are
    ended;"
And, with light in her looks, she entered the chambers
    of sickness.
Noiselessly moved about the assiduous, careful attendants,
Moistening the feverish lip, and the aching brow, and
    in silence
Closing the sightless eyes of the dead, and concealing
    their faces,
Where on their pallets they lay, like drifts of snow by
    the roadside.
Many a languid head, upraised as Evangeline entered,
Turned on its pillow of pain to gaze while she passed,
    for her presence
Fell on their hearts like a ray of the sun on the walls
    of a prison.
And, as she looked around, she saw how Death, the
    consoler,
Laying his hand upon many a heart, had healed it
    forever.
Many familiar forms had disappeared in the nighttime;
Vacant their places were, or filled already by strangers.

Suddenly, as if arrested by fear or a feeling of wonder,
Still she stood, with her colorless lips apart, while a
    shudder
Ran through her frame, and, forgotten, the flowerets
    dropped from her fingers,
And from her eyes and cheeks the light and bloom
    of the morning.
Then there escaped from her lips a cry of such terrible
    anguish,
That the dying heard it, and started up from their
    pillows.
On the pallet before her was stretched the form of an
    old man.
Long, and thin, and gray were the locks that shaded
    his temples;
But, as he lay in the morning light, his face for a
    moment
Seemed to assume once more the forms of its earlier
    manhood;
So are wont to be changed the faces of those who
    are dying.
Hot and red on his lips still burned the flush of the
    fever,
As if life, like the Hebrew, with blood had besprinkled
    its portals,
That the Angel of Death might see the sign, and pass
    over.
Motionless, senseless, dying, he lay, and his spirit
    exhausted
Seemed to be sinking down through infinite depths in
    the darkness,
Darkness of slumber and death, forever sinking and
    sinking.
Then through those realms of shade, in multiplied
    reverberations,

Heard he that cry of pain, and through the hush that
    succeeded
Whispered a gentle voice, in accents tender and saintlike,
"Gabriel! O my beloved!" and died away into silence.
Then he beheld, in a dream, once more the home of
    his childhood;
Green Acadian meadows, with sylvan rivers among them,
Village, and mountain, and woodlands; and walking
    under their shadow,
As in the days of her youth, Evangeline rose in his
    vision.
Tears came into his eyes; and as slowly he lifted his
    eyelids,
Vanished the vision away, but Evangeline knelt by his
    bedside.
Vainly he strove to whisper her name, for the accents
    unuttered
Died on his lips, and their motion revealed what his
    tongue would have spoken.
Vainly he strove to rise; and Evangeline, kneeling beside
    him,
Kissed his dying lips, and laid his head on her bosom.
Sweet was the light of his eyes; but it suddenly sank
    into darkness,
As when a lamp is blown out by a gust of wind at
    a casement.

All was ended now, the hope, and the fear, and the
    sorrow,
All the aching of heart, the restless, unsatisfied longing,
All the dull, deep pain, and constant anguish of patience!
And, as she pressed once more the lifeless head to her
    bosom,
Meekly she bowed her own, and murmured, "Father,
    I thank thee!"

Still stands the forest primeval; but far away from its
    shadow,
Side by side, in their nameless graves, the lovers are
    sleeping.
Under the humble walls of the little Catholic churchyard,
In the heart of the city, they lie, unknown and unnoticed.
Daily the tides of life go ebbing and flowing beside
    them,
Thousands of throbbing hearts, where theirs are at rest
    and forever,
Thousands of aching brains, where theirs no longer are
    busy,
Thousands of toiling hands, where theirs have ceased
    from their labors,
Thousands of weary feet, where theirs have completed
    their journey!

Still stands the forest primeval; but under the shade
    of its branches
Dwells another race, with other customs and language.
Only along the shore of the mournful and misty Atlantic
Linger a few Acadian peasants, whose fathers from exile
Wandered back to their native land to die in its bosom,
In the fisherman's cot the wheel and the loom are still
    busy;
Maidens still wear their Norman caps and their kirtles
    of homespun,
And by the evening fire repeat Evangeline's story,
While from its rocky caverns the deep-voiced, neighboring
    ocean
Speaks, and in accents disconsolate answers the wail of
    the forest.

From
The Song of
Hiawatha

HIAWATHA'S FASTING

You shall hear how Hiawatha
Prayed and fasted in the forest,
Not for greater skill in hunting,
Not for greater craft in fishing,
Not for triumphs in the battle,
And renown among the warriors,
But for profit of the people,
For advantage of the nations.

First he built a lodge for fasting,
Built a wigwam in the forest,
By the shining Big-Sea-Water,
In the blithe and pleasant Springtime,
In the Moon of Leaves he built it,
And, with dreams and visions many,
Seven whole days and nights he fasted.

On the first day of his fasting
Through the leafy woods he wandered;
Saw the deer start from the thicket,
Saw the rabbit in his burrow,
Heard the pheasant, Bena, drumming,
Heard the squirrel, Adjidaumo,
Rattling in his hoard of acorns,
Saw the pigeon, the Omeme,
Building nests among the pine trees,
And in flocks the wild goose, Wawa,
Flying to the fenlands northward,
Whirring, wailing far above him.
"Master of Life!" he cried, desponding,
"Must our lives depend on these things?"

On the next day of his fasting
By the river's brink he wandered,

Through the Muskoday, the meadow,
Saw the wild rice, Mahnomnee,
Saw the blueberry, Meenahga,
And the strawberry, Odahmin,
And the gooseberry, Shahbomin,
And the grapevine, the Bemahgut,
Trailing o'er the alder branches,
Filling all the air with fragrance!
"Master of Life!" he cried, desponding,
"Must our lives depend on these things?"
    On the third day of his fasting
By the lake he sat and pondered,
By the still, transparent water;
Saw the sturgeon, Nahma, leaping,
Scattering drops like beads of wampum,
Saw the yellow perch, the Sahwa,
Like a sunbeam in the water,
Saw the pike, the Maskenozha,
And the herring, Okahahwis,
And the Shawgashee, the crawfish!
"Master of Life!" he cried, desponding,
"Must our lives depend on these things?"
    On the fourth day of his fasting
In his lodge he lay exhausted;
From his couch of leaves and branches
Gazing with half-open eyelids,
Full of shadowy dreams and visions,
On the dizzy, swimming landscape,
On the gleaming of the water,
On the splendor of the sunset.
And he saw a youth approaching,
Dressed in garments green and yellow
Coming through the purple twilight,
Through the splendor of the sunset;
Plumes of green bent o'er his forehead,
And his hair was soft and golden.

Standing at the open doorway,
Long he looked at Hiawatha,
Looked with pity and compassion
On his wasted form and features,
And, in accents like the sighing
Of the South-Wind in the treetops,
Said he, "O my Hiawatha!
All your prayers are heard in heaven,
For you pray not like the others;
Not for greater skill in hunting,
Not for greater craft in fishing,
Not for triumph in the battle,
Nor renown among the warriors,
But for profit of the people,
For advantage of the nations.

   "From the Master of Life descending,
I, the friend of man, Mondamin,
Come to warn you and instruct you,
How by struggle and by labor
You shall gain what you have prayed for.
Rise up from your bed of branches,
Rise, O youth, and wrestle with me!"

   Faint with famine, Hiawatha
Started from his bed of branches,
From the twilight of his wigwam
Forth into the flush of sunset
Came, and wrestled with Mondamin;
At his touch he felt new courage
Throbbing in his brain and bosom,
Felt new life and hope and vigor
Run through every nerve and fiber
So they wrestled there together
In the glory of the sunset,
And the more they strove and struggled,
Stronger still grew Hiawatha;

Till the darkness fell around them,
And the heron, the Shuh-shuh-gah,
From her nest among the pine trees,
Gave a cry of lamentation,
Gave a scream of pain and famine.
   " 'T is enough!" then said Mondamin,
Smiling upon Hiawatha,
"But tomorrow, when the sun sets,
I will come again to try you."
And he vanished, and was seen not;
Whether sinking as the rain sinks,
Whether rising as the mists rise,
Hiawatha saw not, knew not,
Only saw that he had vanished,
Leaving him alone and fainting,
With the misty lake below him,
And the reeling stars above him.
   On the morrow and the next day,
When the sun through heaven descending,
Like a red and burning cinder
From the hearth of the Great Spirit,
Fell into the western waters,
Came Mondamin for the trial,
For the strife with Hiawatha;
Came as silent as the dew comes,
From the empty air appearing,
Into empty air returning,
Taking shape when earth it touches,
But invisible to all men
In its coming and its going.
   Thrice they wrestled there together
In the glory of the sunset,
Till the darkness fell around them,
Till the heron, the Shuh-shuh-gah,
From her nest among the pine trees,

Uttered her loud cry of famine,
And Mondamin paused to listen.

Tall and beautiful he stood there,
In his garments green and yellow;
To and fro his plumes above him
Waved and nodded with his breathing,
And the sweat of the encounter
Stood like drops of dew upon him.

And he cried, "O Hiawatha!
Bravely have you wrestled with me,
Thrice have wrestled stoutly with me,
And the Master of Life, who sees us,
He will give to you the triumph!"

Then he smiled, and said: "Tomorrow
Is the last day of your conflict,
Is the last day of your fasting.
You will conquer and o'ercome me;
Make a bed for me to lie in,
Where the rain may fall upon me,
Where the sun may come and warm me;
Strip these garments, green and yellow,
Strip this nodding plumage from me,
Lay me in the earth, and make it
Soft and loose and light above me.

"Let no hand disturb my slumber,
Let no weed nor worm molest me,
Let not Kahgahgee, the raven,
Come to haunt me and molest me,
Only come yourself to watch me,
Till I wake, and start, and quicken,
Till I leap into the sunshine."

And thus saying, he departed;
Peacefully slept Hiawatha,
But he heard the Wawonaissa,
Heard the whippoorwill complaining,

Perched upon his lonely wigwam;
Heard the rushing Sebowisha,
Heard the rivulet rippling near him,
Talking to the darksome forest;
Heard the sighing of the branches,
As they lifted and subsided
At the passing of the Night-Wind,
Heard them, as one hears in slumber
Far-off murmurs, dreamy whispers:
Peacefully slept Hiawatha.

On the morrow came Nokomis,
On the seventh day of his fasting,
Came with food for Hiawatha,
Came imploring and bewailing,
Lest his hunger should o'ercome him,
Lest his fasting should be fatal.

But he tasted not, and touched not,
Only said to her, "Nokomis,
Wait until the sun is setting,
Till the darkness falls around us,
Till the heron, the Shuh-shuh-gah,
Crying from the desolate marshes,
Tells us that the day is ended."

Homeward weeping went Nokomis,
Sorrowing for her Hiawatha,
Fearing lest his strength should fail him,
Lest his fasting should be fatal.
He meanwhile sat weary waiting
For the coming of Mondamin,
Till the shadows, pointing eastward,
Lengthened over field and forest,
Till the sun dropped from the heaven,
Floating on the waters westward,
As a red leaf in the Autumn
Falls and floats upon the water,
Falls and sinks into its bosom.

And behold! the young Mondamin,
With his soft and shining tresses,
With his garments green and yellow,
With his long and glossy plumage,
Stood and beckoned at the doorway.
And as one in slumber walking,
Pale and haggard, but undaunted,
From the wigwam Hiawatha
Came and wrestled with Mondamin.

Round about him spun the landscape,
Sky and forest reeled together,
And his strong heart leaped within him,
As the sturgeon leaps and struggles
In a net to break its meshes.
Like a ring of fire around him
Blazed and flared the red horizon,
And a hundred suns seemed looking
At the combat of the wrestlers.

Suddenly upon the greensward
All alone stood Hiawatha,
Panting with his wild exertion,
Palpitating with the struggle;
And before him breathless, lifeless,
Lay the youth, with hair dishevelled,
Plumage torn, and garments tattered,
Dead he lay there in the sunset.

And victorious Hiawatha
Made the grave as he commanded,
Stripped the garments from Mondamin,
Stripped his tattered plumage from him,
Laid him in the earth, and made it
Soft and loose and light above him;
And the heron, the Shuh-shuh-gah,
From the melancholy moorlands,
Gave a cry of lamentation,
Gave a cry of pain and anguish!

Homeward then went Hiawatha
To the lodge of old Nokomis,
And the seven days of his fasting
Were accomplished and completed.
But the place was not forgotten
Where he wrestled with Mondamin;
Nor forgotten nor neglected
Was the grave where lay Mondamin,
Sleeping in the rain and sunshine,
Where his scattered plumes and garments
Faded in the rain and sunshine.

Day by day did Hiawatha
Go to wait and watch beside it;
Kept the dark mould soft above it,
Kept it clean from weeds and insects,
Drove away, with scoffs and shoutings,
Kahgahgee, the king of ravens.

Till at length a small green feather
From the earth shot slowly upward,
Then another and another,
And before the Summer ended
Stood the maize in all its beauty,
With its shining robes about it,
And its long, soft, yellow tresses;
And in rapture Hiawatha
Cried aloud, "It is Mondamin!
Yes, the friend of man, Mondamin!"

Then he called to old Nokomis
And Iagoo, the great boaster,
Showed them where the maize was growing,
Told them of his wondrous vision,
Of his wrestling and his triumph,
Of this new gift to the nations,
Which should be their food forever.

And still later, when the Autumn
Changed the long, green leaves to yellow,
And the soft and juicy kernels
Grew like wampum hard and yellow,
Then the ripened ears he gathered,
Stripped the withered husks from off them,
As he once had stripped the wrestler,
Gave the first Feast of Mondamin,
And made known unto the people
This new gift of the Great Spirit.

HIAWATHA'S DEPARTURE

By the shore of Gitche Gumee,
By the shining Big-Sea-Water,
At the doorway of his wigwam,
In the pleasant Summer morning,
Hiawatha stood and waited.
All the air was full of freshness,
All the earth was bright and joyous,
And before him, through the sunshine,
Westward toward the neighboring forest
Passed in golden swarms the Ahmo,
Passed the bees, the honeymakers,
Burning, singing in the sunshine.

Bright above him shone the heavens,
Level spread the lake before him;
From its bosom leaped the sturgeon,
Sparkling, flashing in the sunshine;
On its margin the great forest
Stood reflected in the water,
Every treetop had its shadow,
Motionless beneath the water.

From the brow of Hiawatha
Gone was every trace of sorrow,
As the fog from off the water,
As the mist from off the meadow.
With a smile of joy and triumph,
With a look of exultation,
As of one who in a vision
Sees what is to be, but is not,
Stood and waited Hiawatha.

Toward the sun his hands were lifted,
Both the palms spread out against it,
And between the parted fingers

Fell the sunshine on his features,
Flecked with light his naked shoulders,
As it falls and flecks an oak tree
Through the rifted leaves and branches.
    O'er the water floating, flying,
Something in the hazy distance,
Something in the mists of morning,
Loomed and lifted from the water,
Now seemed floating, now seemed flying,
Coming nearer, nearer, nearer.
    Was it Shingebis the diver?
Or the pelican, the Shada?
Or the heron, the Shuh-shuh-gah?
Or the white goose, Waw-be-wawa,
With the water dripping, flashing,
From its glossy neck and feathers?
    It was neither goose nor diver,
Neither pelican nor heron,
O'er the water floating, flying,
Through the shining mist of morning,
But a birch canoe with paddles,
Rising, sinking on the water,
Dripping, flashing in the sunshine;
And within it came a people
From the distant land of Wabun,
From the farthest realms of morning
Came the Black-Robe chief, the Prophet,
He the Priest of Prayer, the Paleface,
With his guides and his companions.
    And the noble Hiawatha,
With his hands aloft extended,
Held aloft in sign of welcome,
Waited, full of exultation
Till the birch canoe with paddles
Grated on the shining pebbles,
Stranded on the sandy margin,

Till the Black-Robe chief, the Paleface,
With the cross upon his bosom,
Landed on the sandy margin.
  Then the joyous Hiawatha
Cried aloud and spake in this wise:
"Beautiful is the sun, O strangers,
When you come so far to see us!
All our town in peace awaits you,
All our doors stand open for you;
You shall enter all our wigwams,
For the heart's right hand we give you.
  "Never bloomed the earth so gaily,
Never shone the sun so brightly,
As today they shine and blossom
When you come so far to see us!
Never was our lake so tranquil,
Nor so free from rocks and sandbars;
For your birch canoe in passing
Has removed both rock and sandbar.
  "Never before had our tobacco
Such a sweet and pleasant flavor,
Never the broad leaves of our cornfields
Were so beautiful to look on,
As they seem to us this morning,
When you come so far to see us!"
  And the Black-Robe chief made answer,
Stammered in his speech a little,
Speaking words yet unfamiliar:
"Peace be with you, Hiawatha,
Peace be with you and your people,
Peace of prayer, and peace of pardon,
Peace of Christ, and joy of Mary!"
  Then the generous Hiawatha
Led the strangers to his wigwam,
Seated them on skins of bison,
Seated them on skins of ermine,

And the careful, old Nokomis
Brought them food in bowls of bass-wood,
Water brought in birchen dippers,
And the calumet, the peace pipe,
Filled and lighted for their smoking.
All the old men of the village,
All the warriors of the nation,
All the Jossakeeds, the prophets,
The magicians, the Wabenos,
And the medicine-men, the Medas,
Came to bid the strangers welcome;
"It is well," they said, "O brothers,
That you come so far to see us!"
In a circle round the doorway,
With their pipes they sat in silence,
Waiting to behold the strangers,
Waiting to receive their message;
Till the Black-Robe chief, the Paleface,
From the wigwam came to greet them,
Stammering in his speech a little,
Speaking words yet unfamiliar;
"It is well," they said, "O brother,
That you come so far to see us!"
Then the Black-Robe chief, the prophet,
Told his message to the people,
Told the purport of his mission,
Told them of the Virgin Mary,
And her blessed Son, the Savior,
How in distant lands and ages
He had lived on earth as we do;
How he fasted, prayed and labored;
How the Jews, the tribe accursed,
Mocked him, scourged him, crucified him;
How he rose from where they laid him,
Walked again with his disciples,
And ascended into heaven.

And the chiefs made answer, saying:
"We have listened to your message,
We have heard your words of wisdom,
We will think on what you tell us.
It is well for us, O brothers,
That you come so far to see us!"

Then they rose up and departed
Each one homeward to his wigwam,
To the young men and the women,
Told the story of the strangers
Whom the Master of Life had sent them
From the shining land of Wabun.

Heavy with the heat and silence
Grew the afternoon of Summer;
With a drowsy sound the forest
Whispered round the sultry wigwam,
With a sound of sleep the water
Rippled on the beach below it;
From the cornfields shrill and ceaseless
Sang the grasshopper, Pah-puk-keena;
And the guests of Hiawatha,
Weary with the heat of Summer,
Slumbered in the sultry wigwam.

Slowly o'er the simmering landscape
Fell the evening's dusk and coolness,
And the long and level sunbeams
Shot their spears into the forest,
Breaking through its shields of shadow,
Rushed into each secret ambush,
Searched each thicket, dingle, hollow;
Still the guests of Hiawatha
Slumbered in the silent wigwam.

From his place rose Hiawatha,
Bade farewell to old Nokomis,
Spake in whispers, spake in this wise,
Did not wake the guests, that slumbered:

"I am going, O Nokomis,
On a long and distant journey,
To the portals of the Sunset,
To the regions of the home-wind,
Of the Northwest wind, Keewaydin.
But these guests I leave behind me,
In your watch and ward I leave them;
See that never harm comes near them,
See that never fear molests them,
Never danger nor suspicion,
Never want of food or shelter,
In the lodge of Hiawatha!"

Forth into the village went he,
Bade farewell to all the warriors,
Bade farewell to all the young men,
Spake persuading, spake in this wise:
"I am going, O my people,
On a long and distant journey;
Many moons and many winters
Will have come, and will have vanished
Ere I come again to see you.
But my guests I leave behind me;
Listen to their words of wisdom,
Listen to the truth they tell you,
For the Master of Life has sent them
From the land of light and morning!"

On the shore stood Hiawatha,
Turned and waved his hand at parting;
On the clear and luminous water
Launched his birch canoe for sailing,
From the pebbles of the margin
Shoved it forth into the water;
Whispered to it, "Westward! westward!"
And with speed it darted forward.

And the evening sun descending
Set the clouds on fire with redness,

Burned the broad sky like a prairie,
Left upon the level water
One long track and trail of splendor,
Down whose stream, as down a river,
Westward, westward Hiawatha
Sailed into the fiery sunset,
Sailed into the purple vapors,
Sailed into the dusk of evening.

And the people from the margin
Watched him floating, rising, sinking,
Till the birch canoe seemed lifted
High into that sea of splendor,
Till it sank into the vapors
Like the new moon slowly, slowly
Sinking in the purple distance.

And they said, "Farewell forever!"
Said, "Farewell, O Hiawatha!"
And the forests, dark and lonely,
Moved through all their depths of darkness,
Sighed, "Farewell, O Hiawatha!"
And the waves upon the margin
Rising, rippling on the pebbles,
Sobbed, "Farewell, O Hiawatha!"
And the heron, the Shuh-shuh-gah,
From her haunts among the fenlands,
Screamed, "Farewell, O Hiawatha!"

Thus departed Hiawatha,
Hiawatha the Beloved,
In the glory of the sunset,
In the purple mists of evening,
To the regions of the home-wind,
Of the Northwest wind Keewaydin,
To the Islands of the Blessed,
To the kingdom of Ponemah,
To the land of the Hereafter!

The Courtship
of Miles Standish

I

MILES STANDISH

In the Old Colony days, in Plymouth the land of the
Pilgrims,
To and fro in a room of his simple and primitive
dwelling,
Clad in doublet and hose, and boots of Cordovan leather,
Strode, with a martial air, Miles Standish the Puritan
Captain.
Buried in thought he seemed, with his hands behind
him, and pausing
Ever and anon to behold his glittering weapons of
warfare,
Hanging in shining array along the walls of the chamber,—
Cutlass and corselet of steel, and his trusty sword of
Damascus,
Curved at the point and inscribed with its mystical
Arabic sentence,
While underneath, in a corner, were fowling-piece,
musket, and matchlock.
Short of stature he was, but strongly built and athletic,
Broad in the shoulders, deep-chested, with muscles and
sinews of iron;
Brown as a nut was his face, but his russet beard was
already
Flaked with patches of snow, as hedges sometimes in
November.
Near him was seated John Alden, his friend, and house-
hold companion,
Writing with diligent speed at a table of pine by the
window;
Fair-haired, azure-eyed, with delicate Saxon complexion,

Having the dew of his youth, and the beauty thereof, as the captives
Whom Saint Gregory saw, and exclaimed, "Not Angles, but Angels."
Youngest of all was he of the men who came in the *Mayflower*.

Suddenly breaking the silence, the diligent scribe interrupting,
Spake, in the pride of his heart, Miles Standish the Captain of Plymouth.
"Look at these arms," he said, "the warlike weapons that hang here
Burnished and bright and clean, as if for parade or inspection!
This is the sword of Damascus I fought with in Flanders; this breastplate,
Well I remember the day! once saved my life in a skirmish;
Here in front you can see the very dint of the bullet
Fired point-blank at my heart by a Spanish arcabucero.
Had it not been of sheer steel, the forgotten bones of Miles Standish
Would at this moment be mould, in their grave in the Flemish morasses."
Thereupon answered John Alden, but looked not up from his writing:
"Truly the breath of the Lord hath slackened the speed of the bullet;
He in his mercy preserved you, to be our shield and our weapon!"
Still the Captain continued, unheeding the words of the stripling:
"See, how bright they are burnished, as if in an arsenal hanging;

That is because I have done it myself, and not left it
     to others.
Serve yourself, would you be well served, is an excellent
     adage;
So I take care of my arms, as you of your pens and
     your inkhorn.
Then, too, there are my soldiers, my great, invincible
     army,
Twelve men, all equipped, having each his rest and
     his matchlock,
Eighteen shillings a month, together with diet and
     pillage,
And, like Caesar, I know the name of each of my
     soldiers!"
This he said with a smile, that danced in his eyes, as
     the sunbeams
Dance on the waves of the sea, and vanish again in
     a moment.
Alden laughed as he wrote, and still the Captain con-
     tinued:
"Look! you can see from this window my brazen
     howitzer planted
High on the roof of the church, a preacher who speaks
     to the purpose,
Steady, straightforward, and strong, with irresistible logic,
Orthodox, flashing conviction right into the hearts of
     the heathen.
Now we are ready, I think, for any assault of the
     Indians;
Let them come, if they like, and the sooner they try
     it the better,—
Let them come, if they like, be it sagamore, sachem,
     or pow-wow,
Aspinet, Samoset, Corbitant, Squanto, or Tokamaha-
     mon!"

Long at the window he stood, and wistfully gazed
on the landscape,
Washed with a cold gray mist, the vapory breath of
the east wind,
Forest and meadow and hill, and the steel-blue rim of
the ocean,
Lying silent and sad, in the afternoon shadows and
sunshine.
Over his countenance flitted a shadow like those on
the landscape,
Gloom intermingled with light; and his voice was subdued
with emotion,
Tenderness, pity, regret, as after a pause he proceeded:
"Yonder there, on the hill by the sea, lies buried Rose
Standish;
Beautiful rose of love, that bloomed for me by the
wayside!
She was the first to die of all who came in the
Mayflower!
Green above her is growing the field of wheat we have
sown there,
Better to hide from the Indian scouts the graves of
our people,
Lest they should count them and see how many already
have perished!"
Sadly his face he averted, and strode up and down,
and was thoughtful.

Fixed to the opposite wall was a shelf of books, and
among them
Prominent three, distinguished alike for bulk and for
binding;
Bariffe's Artillery Guide, and the Commentaries of Cæsar
Out of the Latin translated by Arthur Goldinge of
London,

And, as if guarded by these, between them was standing
the Bible.

Musing a moment before them, Miles Standish paused,
as if doubtful

Which of the three he should choose for his consolation
and comfort,

Whether the wars of the Hebrews, the famous campaigns
of the Romans,

Or the Artillery practice, designed for belligerent Chris-
tians.

Finally down from its shelf he dragged the ponderous
Roman,

Seated himself at the window, and opened the book,
and in silence

Turned o'er the well-worn leaves, where thumb marks
thick on the margin,

Like the trample of feet, proclaimed the battle was
hottest.

Nothing was heard in the room but the hurrying pen
of the stripling,

Busily writing epistles important, to go by the *Mayflower*,

Ready to sail on the morrow, or next day at latest,
God willing!

Homeward bound with the tidings of all that terrible
winter,

Letters written by Alden, and full of the name of
Priscilla!

Full of the name and the fame of the Puritan maiden
Priscilla!

II

LOVE AND FRIENDSHIP

Nothing was heard in the room but the hurrying pen
of the stripling,
Or an occasional sigh from the laboring heart of the
Captain,
Reading the marvellous words and achievements of Julius
Caesar.
After a while he exclaimed, as he smote with his hand,
palm downwards,
Heavily on the page: "A wonderful man was this Caesar!
You are a writer, and I am a fighter, but here is a
fellow
Who could both write and fight, and in both was
equally skillful!"
Straightway answered and spake John Alden, the comely,
the youthful:
"Yes, he was equally skilled, as you say, with his pen
and his weapons.
Somewhere have I read, but where I forget, he could
dictate
Seven letters at once, at the same time writing his
memoirs."
"Truly," continued the Captain, not heeding or hearing
the other,
"Truly a wonderful man was Caius Julius Caesar!
Better be first, he said, in a little Iberian village,
Than be second in Rome, and I think he was right
when he said it.
Twice was he married before he was twenty, and many
times after;
Battles five hundred he fought, and a thousand cities
he conquered;
He, too, fought in Flanders, as he himself has recorded;

Finally he was stabbed by his friend, the orator Brutus!
Now, do you know what he did on a certain occasion
    in Flanders,
When the rear-guard of his army retreated, the front
    giving way too,
And the immortal Twelfth Legion was crowded so
    closely together
There was no room for their swords? Why, he seized
    a shield from a soldier,
Put himself straight at the head of his troops, and
    commanded the captains,
Calling on each by his name, to order forward the
    ensigns;
Then to widen the ranks, and give more room for
    their weapons;
So he won the day, the battle of something-or-other.
That's what I always say; if you wish a thing to be
    well done,
You must do it yourself, you must not leave it to
    others!"

All was silent again; the Captain continued his reading.
Nothing was heard in the room but the hurrying pen
    of the stripling
Writing epistles important to go next day by the
    Mayflower,
Filled with the name and the fame of the Puritan maiden
    Priscilla;
Every sentence began or closed with the name of Priscilla,
Till the treacherous pen, to which he confided the secret,
Strove to betray it by singing and shouting the name
    of Priscilla!
Finally closing his book, with a bang of the ponderous
    cover,
Sudden and loud as the sound of a soldier grounding
    his musket,

Thus to the young man spake Miles Standish the Captain
of Plymouth:
"When you have finished your work, I have something
important to tell you.
Be not, however, in haste; I can wait; I shall not be
impatient!"
Straightway Alden replied, as he folded the last of his
letters,
Pushing his papers aside, and giving respectful attention:
"Speak; for whenever you speak, I am always ready
to listen,
Always ready to hear whatever pertains to Miles Stand-
ish."
Thereupon answered the Captain, embarrassed, and cull-
ing his phrases:
" 'T is not good for a man to be alone, say the
Scriptures.
This I have said before, and again and again I repeat
it:
Every hour in the day, I think it, and feel it, and say it.
Since Rose Standish died, my life has been weary and
dreary;
Sick at heart have I been, beyond the healing of friend-
ship;
Oft in my lonely hours have I thought of the maiden
Priscilla.
She is alone in the world; her father and mother and
brother
Died in the winter together; I saw her going and
coming,
Now to the grave of the dead, and now to the bed
of the dying,
Patient, courageous, and strong, and said to myself,
that if ever
There were angels on earth, as there are angels in
heaven,

Two have I seen and known; and the angel whose
    name is Priscilla
Holds in my desolate life the place which the other
    abandoned.
Long have I cherished the thought, but never have
    dared to reveal it,
Being a coward in this, though valiant enough for the
    most part.
Go to the damsel Priscilla, the loveliest maiden of
    Plymouth,
Say that a blunt old Captain, a man not of words but
    of actions,
Offers his hand and his heart, the hand and heart of
    a soldier.
Not in these words, you know, but this in short is
    my meaning;
I am a maker of war, and not a maker of phrases.
You, who are bred as a scholar, can say it in elegant
    language,
Such as you read in your books of the pleadings and
    wooings of lovers,
Such as you think best adapted to win the heart of
    a maiden."

When he had spoken, John Alden, the fair-haired,
    taciturn stripling,
All aghast at his words, surprised, embarrassed, bewil-
    dered,
Trying to mask his dismay by treating the subject with
    lightness,
Trying to smile, and yet feeling his heart stand still
    in his bosom,
Just as a timepiece stops in a house that is stricken
    by lightning,
Thus made answer and spake, or rather stammered than
    answered:

"Such a message as that, I am sure I should mangle
        and mar it;
If you would have it well done,—I am only repeating
        your maxim,—
You must do it yourself, you must not leave it to
        others!"
But with the air of a man whom nothing can turn
        from his purpose,
Gravely shaking his head, made answer the Captain of
        Plymouth:
"Truly the maxim is good, and I do not mean to
        gainsay it;
But we must use it discreetly, and not waste powder
        for nothing.
Now, as I said before, I was never a maker of phrases.
I can march up to a fortress and summon the place
        to surrender,
But march up to a woman with such a proposal, I
        dare not.
I'm not afraid of bullets, nor shot from the mouth of
        a cannon,
But of a thundering 'No!' point-blank from the mouth
        of a woman,
That I confess I'm afraid of, nor am I ashamed to
        confess it!
So you must grant my request, for you are an elegant
        scholar,
Having the graces of speech, and skill in the turning
        of phrases."
Taking the hand of his friend, who still was reluctant
        and doubtful,
Holding it long in his own, and pressing it kindly,
        he added:
"Though I have spoken thus lightly, yet deep is the
        feeling that prompts me;

Surely you cannot refuse what I ask in the name of
our friendship!"
Then made answer John Alden: "The name of friendship
is sacred;
What you demand in that name, I have not the power
to deny you!"
So the strong will prevailed, subduing and molding
the gentler,
Friendship prevailed over love, and Alden went on his
errand.

III

THE LOVER'S ERRAND

So the strong will prevailed, and Alden went on his
errand,
Out of the street of the village, and into the paths of
the forest,
Into the tranquil woods, where bluebirds and robins
were building
Towns in the populous trees, with hanging gardens of
verdure,
Peaceful, aerial cities of joy and affection and freedom.
All around him was calm, but within him commotion
and conflict,
Love contending with friendship, and self with each
generous impulse.
To and fro in his breast his thoughts were heaving
and dashing,
As in a foundering ship, with every roll of the vessel,
Washes the bitter sea, the merciless surge of the ocean!
"Must I relinquish it all," he cried with a wild lamenta-
tion,—
"Must I relinquish it all, the joy, the hope, the illusion?

Was it for this I have loved, and waited, and worshipped
in silence?
Was it for this I have followed the flying feet and the
shadow
Over the wintry sea, to the desolate shores of New
England?
Truly the heart is deceitful, and out of its depths of
corruption
Rise, like an exhalation, the misty phantoms of passion;
Angels of light they seem, but are only delusions of
Satan.
All is clear to me now; I feel it, I see it distinctly!
This is the hand of the Lord; it is laid upon me in
anger,
For I have followed too much the heart's desires and
devices,
Worshipping Astaroth blindly, and impious idols of Baal.
This is the cross I must bear; the sin and the swift
retribution."

So through the Plymouth woods John Alden went
on his errand;
Crossing the brook at the ford, where it brawled over
pebble and shallow,
Gathering still, as he went, the mayflowers blooming
around him,
Fragrant, filling the air with a strange and wonderful
sweetness,
Children lost in the woods, and covered with leaves
in their slumber.
"Puritan flowers," he said, "and the type of Puritan
maidens,
Modest and simple and sweet, the very type of Priscilla!
So I will take them to her; to Priscilla the mayflower
of Plymouth,

Modest and simple and sweet, as a parting gift will
    I take them;
Breathing their silent farewells, as they fade and wither
    and perish,
Soon to be thrown away as is the heart of the giver."
So through the Plymouth woods John Alden went on
    his errand;
Came to an open space, and saw the disk of the ocean,
Sailless, somber and cold with the comfortless breath
    of the east wind:
Saw the new-built house, and people at work in a meadow;
Heard, as he drew near the door, the musical voice
    of Priscilla
Singing the hundredth psalm, the grand old Puritan
    anthem,
Music that Luther sang to the sacred words of the
    psalmist,
Full of the breath of the Lord, consoling and comforting
    many.
Then, as he opened the door, he beheld the form of
    the maiden
Seated beside her wheel, and the carded wool like a
    snowdrift
Piled at her knee, her white hands feeding the ravenous
    spindle,
While with her foot on the treadle she guided the wheel
    in its motion.
Open wide on her lap lay the well-worn psalm book
    of Ainsworth,
Printed in Amsterdam, the words and the music together,
Rough-hewn, angular notes, like stones in the wall of
    a churchyard,
Darkened and overhung by the running vine of the
    verses.
Such was the book from whose pages she sang the
    old Puritan anthem,

She, the Puritan girl, in the solitude of the forest,
Making the humble house and the modest apparel of
    homespun
Beautiful with her beauty, and rich with the wealth
    of her being!
Over him rushed, like a wind that is keen and cold
    and relentless,
Thoughts of what might have been, and the weight
    and woe of his errand;
All the dreams that had faded, and all the hopes that
    had vanished,
All his life henceforth a dreary and tenantless mansion,
Haunted by vain regrets, and pallid, sorrowful faces.
Still he said to himself, and almost fiercely he said it,
"Let not him that putteth his hand to the plough look
    backwards;
Though the ploughshare cut through the flowers of life
    to its fountains,
Though it pass o'er the graves of the dead and the
    hearths of the living,
It is the will of the Lord; and his mercy endureth forever!"

So he entered the house: and the hum of the wheel
    and the singing
Suddenly ceased; for Priscilla, aroused by his step on
    the threshold,
Rose as he entered, and gave him her hand, in signal
    of welcome,
Saying, "I knew it was you, when I heard your step
    in the passage;
For I was thinking of you, as I sat there singing and
    spinning."
Awkward and dumb with delight, that a thought of
    him had been mingled
Thus in the sacred psalm, that came from the heart
    of the maiden,

Silent before her he stood, and gave her the flowers
     for an answer,
Finding no words for his thought. He remembered that
     day in the winter,
After the first great snow, when he broke a path from
     the village,
Reeling and plunging along through the drifts that
     encumbered the doorway,
Stamping the snow from his feet as he entered the
     house, and Priscilla
Laughed at his snowy locks, and gave him a seat by
     the fireside,
Grateful and pleased to know he had thought of her
     in the snowstorm.
Had he but spoken then! perhaps not in vain had he
     spoken;
Now it was all too late; the golden moment had
     vanished!
So he stood there abashed, and gave her the flowers
     for an answer.

Then they sat down and talked of the birds and the
     beautiful springtime,
Talked of their friends at home, and the *Mayflower*
     that sailed on the morrow.
"I have been thinking all day," said gently the Puritan
     maiden,
"Dreaming all night, and thinking all day, of the hedge-
     rows of England,—
They are in blossom now, and the country is all like
     a garden;
Thinking of lanes and fields, and the song of the lark
     and the linnet,
Seeing the village street, and familiar faces of neighbors
Going about as of old, and stopping to gossip together,

And, at the end of the street, the village church, with
    the ivy
Climbing the old gray tower, and the quiet graves in
    the churchyard.
Kind are the people I live with, and dear to me my
    religion;
Still my heart is so sad, that I wish myself back in
    Old England.
You will say it is wrong, but I cannot help it: I almost
Wish myself back in Old England, I feel so lonely and
    wretched."

Thereupon answered the youth: "Indeed I do not
    condemn you;
Stouter hearts than a woman's have quailed in this
    terrible winter.
Yours is tender and trusting, and needs a stronger to
    lean on;
So I have come to you now, with an offer and proffer
    of marriage
Made by a good man and true, Miles Standish the
    Captain of Plymouth!"

Thus he delivered his message, the dexterous writer
    of letters,—
Did not embellish the theme, nor array it in beautiful
    phrases,
But came straight to the point, and blurted it out like
    a schoolboy;
Even the Captain himself could hardly have said it more
    bluntly.
Mute with amazement and sorrow, Priscilla the Puritan
    maiden
Looked into Alden's face, her eyes dilated with wonder,
Feeling his words like a blow, that stunned her and
    rendered her speechless;

Till at length she exclaimed, interrupting the ominous
  silence:
"If the great Captain of Plymouth is so very eager to
  wed me,
Why does he not come himself, and take the trouble
  to woo me?
If I am not worth the wooing, I surely am not worth
  the winning!"
Then John Alden began explaining and smoothing the
  matter,
Making it worse as he went, by saying the Captain
  was busy,—
Had no time for such things;—such things! the words
  grating harshly
Fell on the ear of Priscilla; and swift as a flash she
  made answer:
"Has he no time for such things, as you call it, before
  he is married,
Would he be likely to find it, or make it, after the
  wedding?
That is the way with you men; you don't understand
  us, you cannot.
When you have made up your minds, after thinking
  of this one and that one,
Choosing, selecting, rejecting, comparing one with an-
  other,
Then you make known your desire, with abrupt and
  sudden avowal,
And are offended and hurt, and indignant, perhaps, that
  a woman
Does not respond at once to a love that she never
  suspected,
Does not attain at a bound the height to which you
  have been climbing.
This is not right nor just: for surely a woman's affection

Is not a thing to be asked for, and had for only the
asking.
When one is truly in love, one not only says it, but
shows it.
Had he but waited a while, had he only showed that
he loved me,
Even this Captain of yours—who knows?—at last might
have won me,
Old and rough as he is; but now it never can happen."

Still John Alden went on, unheeding the words of
Priscilla,
Urging the suit of his friend, explaining, persuading,
expanding;
Spoke of his courage and skill, and of all his battles
in Flanders,
How with the people of God he had chosen to suffer
affliction;
How, in return for his zeal, they had made him Captain
of Plymouth;
He was a gentleman born, could trace his pedigree
plainly
Back to Hugh Standish of Duxbury Hall, in Lancashire,
England,
Who was the son of Ralph, and the grandson of Thurston
de Standish;
Heir unto vast estates, of which he was basely defrauded,
Still bore the family arms, and had for his crest a cock
argent
Combed and wattled gules, and all the rest of the
blazon.
He was a man of honor, of noble and generous nature;
Though he was rough, he was kindly; she knew how
during the winter
He had attended the sick, with a hand as gentle as
woman's;

Somewhat hasty and hot, he could not deny it, and
    headstrong,
Stern as a soldier might be, but hearty, and placable
    always,
Not to be laughed at and scorned, because he was little
    of stature;
For he was great of heart, magnanimous, courtly,
    courageous;
Any woman in Plymouth, nay, any woman in England,
Might be happy and proud to be called the wife of
    Miles Standish!

But as he warmed and glowed, in his simple and
    eloquent language,
Quite forgetful of self, and full of the praise of his
    rival,
Archly the maiden smiled, and, with eyes overrunning
    with laughter,
Said, in a tremulous voice, "Why don't you speak for
    yourself, John?"

IV

JOHN ALDEN

Into the open air John Alden, perplexed and bewildered,
Rushed like a man insane, and wandered alone by the
    seaside;
Paced up and down the sands, and bared his head to
    the east wind,
Cooling his heated brow, and the fire and fever within
    him.
Slowly as out of the heavens, with apocalyptical splendors,
Sank the City of God, in the vision of John the Apostle,

So, with its cloudy walls of chrysolite, jasper, and
      sapphire,
Sank the broad red sun, and over its turrets uplifted
Glimmered the golden reed of the angel who measured
      the city.

"Welcome, O wind of the East!" he exclaimed in
      his wild exultation,
"Welcome, O wind of the East, from the caves of the
      misty Atlantic!
Blowing o'er fields of dulse, and measureless meadows
      of sea grass,
Blowing o'er rocky wastes, and the grottos and gardens
      of ocean!
Lay thy cold, moist hand on my burning forehead,
      and wrap me
Close in thy garments of mist, to allay the fever within
      me!"

Like an awakened conscience, the sea was moaning
      and tossing,
Beating remorseful and loud the mutable sands of the
      seashore.
Fierce in his soul was the struggle and tumult of passions
      contending;
Love triumphant and crowned, and friendship wounded
      and bleeding,
Passionate cries of desire, and importunate pleadings of
      duty!
"Is it my fault," he said, "that the maiden has chosen
      between us?
Is it my fault that he failed,—my fault that I am the
      victor?"
Then within him there thundered a voice, like the voice
      of the Prophet:

"It hath displeased the Lord!"—and he thought of David's
    transgression,
Bathsheba's beautiful face, and his friend in the front
    of the battle!
Shame and confusion of guilt, and abasement and self-
    condemnation,
Overwhelmed him at once; and he cried in the deepest
    contrition:
"It hath displeased the Lord! It is the temptation of
    Satan!"

Then, uplifting his head, he looked at the sea, and
    beheld there
Dimly the shadowy form of the *Mayflower* riding at
    anchor,
Rocked on the rising tide, and ready to sail on the
    morrow;
Heard the voices of men through the mist, the rattle
    of cordage
Thrown on the deck, the shouts of the mate, and the
    sailors' "Ay, ay, Sir!"
Clear and distinct, but not loud, in the dripping air
    of the twilight.
Still for a moment he stood, and listened, and stared
    at the vessel,
Then went hurriedly on, as one who, seeing a phantom,
Stops, then quickens his pace, and follows the beckoning
    shadow.
"Yes, it is plain to me now," he murmured; "the hand
    of the Lord is
Leading me out of the land of darkness, the bondage
    of error,
Through the sea, that shall lift the walls of its waters
    around me,
Hiding me, cutting me off, from the cruel thoughts
    that pursue me.

Back will I go o'er the ocean, this dreary land will
    abandon,
Her whom I may not love, and him whom my heart
    has offended.
Better to be in my grave in the green old churchyard
    in England,
Close by my mother's side, and among the dust of
    my kindred;
Better be dead and forgotten, than living in shame and
    dishonor;
Sacred and safe and unseen, in the dark of the narrow
    chamber
With me my secret shall lie, like a buried jewel that
    glimmers
Bright on the hand that is dust, in the chambers of
    silence and darkness,—
Yes, as the marriage ring of the great espousal hereafter!"

Thus as he spake, he turned, in the strength of his
    strong resolution,
Leaving behind him the shore, and hurried along in
    the twilight,
Through the congenial gloom of the forest silent and
    somber,
Till he beheld the lights in the seven houses of Plymouth,
Shining like seven stars in the dusk and mist of the
    evening.
Soon he entered his door, and found the redoubtable
    Captain
Sitting alone, and absorbed in the martial pages of
    Caesar,
Fighting some great campaign in Hainault or Brabant
    or Flanders.
"Long have you been on your errand," he said with
    a cheery demeanor,

Even as one who is waiting an answer, and fears not
    the issue.
"Not far off is the house, although the woods are
    between us;
But you have lingered so long, that while you were
    going and coming
I have fought ten battles and sacked and demolished
    a city.
Come, sit down, and in order relate to me all that
    has happened."

Then John Alden spake, and related the wondrous
    adventure,
From beginning to end, minutely, just as it happened;
How he had seen Priscilla, and how he had sped in
    his courtship,
Only smoothing a little, and softening down her refusal.
But when he came at length to the words Priscilla had
    spoken,
Words so tender and cruel: "Why don't you speak for
    yourself, John?"
Up leaped the Captain of Plymouth, and stamped on
    the floor, till his armor
Clanged on the wall, where it hung, with a sound of
    sinister omen.
All his pent-up wrath burst forth in a sudden explosion,
E'en as a hand grenade, that scatters destruction around
    it.
Wildly he shouted, and loud: "John Alden! you have
    betrayed me!
Me, Miles Standish, your friend! have supplanted, de-
    frauded, betrayed me!
One of my ancestors ran his sword through the heart
    of Wat Tyler;
Who shall prevent me from running my own through
    the heart of a traitor?

Yours is the greater treason, for yours is a treason to
      friendship!
You, who lived under my roof, whom I cherished and
      loved as a brother;
You, who have fed at my board, and drunk at my
      cup, to whose keeping
I have intrusted my honor, my thoughts the most sacred
      and secret,—
You too, Brutus! ah, woe to the name of friendship
      hereafter!
Brutus was Caesar's friend, and you were mine, but
      henceforward
Let there be nothing between us save war, and implacable
      hatred!"

So spake the Captain of Plymouth, and strode about
      in the chamber,
Chafing and choking with rage; like cords were the
      veins on his temples.
But in the midst of his anger a man appeared at the
      doorway,
Bringing in uttermost haste a message of urgent im-
      portance,
Rumors of danger and war and hostile incursions of
      Indians!
Straightway the Captain paused, and, without further
      question or parley,
Took from the nail on the wall his sword with its
      scabbard of iron,
Buckled the belt round his waist, and, frowning fiercely,
      departed.
Alden was left alone. He heard the clank of the scabbard
Growing fainter and fainter, and dying away in the
      distance.
Then he arose from his seat, and looked forth into
      the darkness,

Felt the cool air blow on his cheek, that was hot with
the insult,
Lifted his eyes to the heavens, and, folding his hands
as in childhood,
Prayed in the silence of night to the Father who seeth
in secret.

Meanwhile the choleric Captain strode wrathful away
to the council,
Found it already assembled, impatiently waiting his
coming;
Men in the middle of life, austere and grave in deportment,
Only one of them old, the hill that was nearest to
heaven,
Covered with snow, but erect, the excellent Elder of
Plymouth.
God had sifted three kingdoms to find the wheat for
this planting,
Then had sifted the wheat, as the living seed of a
nation;
So say the chronicles old, and such is the faith of the
people!
Near them was standing an Indian, in attitude stern
and defiant;
Naked down to the waist, and grim and ferocious in
aspect;
While on the table before them was lying unopened
a Bible,
Ponderous, bound in leather, brass-studded, printed in
Holland,
And beside it outstretched the skin of a rattlesnake
glittered,
Filled, like a quiver, with arrows; a signal and challenge
of warfare,
Brought by the Indian, and speaking with arrowy tongues
of defiance.

This Miles Standish beheld, as he entered, and heard
 them debating
What were an answer befitting the hostile message and
 menace,
Talking of this and of that, contriving, suggesting,
 objecting;
One voice only for peace, and that the voice of the
 Elder,
Judging it wise and well that some at least were converted,
Rather than any were slain, for this was but Christian
 behavior!
Then out spake Miles Standish, the stalwart Captain
 of Plymouth,
Muttering deep in his throat, for his voice was husky
 with anger,
"What do you mean to make war with milk and the
 water of roses?
Is it to shoot red squirrels you have your howitzer
 planted
There on the roof of the church, or is it to shoot red
 devils?
Truly the only tongue that is understood by a savage
Must be the tongue of fire that speaks from the mouth
 of the cannon!"
Thereupon answered and said the excellent Elder of
 Plymouth,
Somewhat amazed and alarmed at this irreverent lan-
 guage:
"Not so thought St. Paul, nor yet the other Apostles;
Not from the cannon's mouth were the tongues of fire
 they spake with!"
But unheeded fell this mild rebuke on the Captain,
Who had advanced to the table, and thus continued
 discoursing:
"Leave this matter to me, for to me by right it
 pertaineth.
War is a terrible trade; but in the cause that is righteous,

Sweet is the smell of powder; and thus I answer the
challenge!"

Then from the rattlesnake's skin, with a sudden,
contemptuous gesture,
Jerking the Indian arrows, he filled it with powder and
bullets
Full to the very jaws, and handed it back to the savage,
Saying, in thundering tones: "Here, take it! this is your
answer!"
Silently out of the room then glided the glistening
savage,
Bearing the serpent's skin, and seeming himself like a
serpent,
Winding his sinuous way in the dark to the depths of
the forest.

V

THE SAILING OF THE *MAYFLOWER*

Just in the gray of the dawn, as the mists uprose from
the meadows,
There was a stir and a sound in the slumbering village
of Plymouth;
Clanging and clicking of arms, and the order imperative,
"Forward!"
Given in tone suppressed, a tramp of feet, and then
silence.
Figures ten, in the mist, marched slowly out of the
village.
Standish the stalwart it was, with eight of his valorous
army,
Led by their Indian guide, by Hobomok, friend of the
white men,

Northward marching to quell the sudden revolt of the
  savage.
Giants they seemed in the mist, or the mighty men
  of King David;
Giants in heart they were, who believed in God and
  the Bible,—
Ay, who believed in the smiting of Midianites and
  Philistines.
Over them gleamed far off the crimson banners of
  morning;
Under them loud on the sands, the serried billows,
  advancing,
Fired along the line, and in regular order retreated.

Many a mile had they marched, when at length the
  village of Plymouth
Woke from its sleep, and arose, intent on its manifold
  labors.
Sweet was the air and soft; and slowly the smoke from
  the chimneys
Rose over roofs of thatch, and pointed steadily east-
  ward;
Men came forth from the doors, and paused and talked
  of the weather,
Said that the wind had changed, and was blowing fair
  for the *Mayflower*;
Talked of their Captain's departure, and all the dangers
  that menaced,
He being gone, the town, and what should be done
  in his absence.
Merrily sang the birds, and the tender voices of women
Consecrated with hymns the common cares of the
  household.
Out of the sea rose the sun, and the billows rejoiced
  at his coming;

Beautiful were his feet on the purple tops of the
    mountains;
Beautiful on the sails of the *Mayflower* riding at anchor,
Battered and blackened and worn by all the storms of
    the winter.
Loosely against her masts was hanging and flapping her
    canvas,
Rent by so many gales, and patched by the hands of
    the sailors.
Suddenly from her side, as the sun rose over the ocean,
Darted a puff of smoke, and floated seaward; anon rang
Loud over field and forest the cannon's roar, and the
    echoes
Heard and repeated the sound, the signal-gun of depar-
    ture!
Ah! but with louder echoes replied the hearts of the
    people!
Meekly, in voices subdued, the chapter was read from
    the Bible,
Meekly the prayer was begun, but ended in fervent
    entreaty!
Then from their houses in haste came forth the Pilgrims
    of Plymouth,
Men and women and children, all hurrying down to
    the seashore,
Eager, with tearful eyes, to say farewell to the *May-
    flower*,
Homeward bound o'er the sea, and leaving them here
    in the desert.

Foremost among them was Alden. All night he had
    lain without slumber,
Turning and tossing about in the heat and unrest of
    his fever.
He had beheld Miles Standish, who came back late
    from the council,

Stalking into the room, and heard him mutter and
    murmur,
Sometimes it seemed a prayer, and sometimes it sounded
    like swearing.
Once he had come to the bed, and stood there a
    moment in silence;
Then he had turned away, and said: "I will not awake
    him;
Let him sleep on, it is best; for what is the use of
    more talking!"
Then he extinguished the light, and threw himself down
    on his pallet,
Dressed as he was, and ready to start at the break of
    the morning,—
Covered himself with the cloak he had worn in his
    campaigns in Flanders,—
Slept as a soldier sleeps in his bivouac, ready for
    action.
But with the dawn he arose; in the twilight Alden
    beheld him
Put on his corselet of steel, and all the rest of his
    armor,
Buckle about his waist his trusty blade of Damascus,
Take from the corner his musket, and so stride out
    of the chamber.
Often the heart of the youth had burned and yearned
    to embrace him,
Often his lips had essayed to speak, imploring for
    pardon;
All the old friendship came back, with its tender and
    grateful emotions;
But his pride overmastered the nobler nature within
    him,—
Pride, and the sense of his wrong, and the burning
    fire of the insult.

So he beheld his friend departing in anger, but spake
     not,
Saw him go forth to danger, perhaps to death, and
     he spake not!
Then he arose from his bed, and heard what the people
     were saying,
Joined in the talk at the door, with Stephen and Richard
     and Gilbert,
Joined in the morning prayer, and in the reading of
     Scripture,
And, with the others, in haste went hurrying down
     to the seashore,
Down to the Plymouth Rock, that had been to their
     feet as a doorstep
Into a world unknown,—the cornerstone of a nation!

There with his boat was the Master, already a little
     impatient
Lest he should lose the tide, or the wind might shift
     to the eastward,
Square-built, hearty, and strong, with an odor of ocean
     about him,
Speaking with this one and that, and cramming letters
     and parcels
Into his pockets capacious, and messages mingled together
Into his narrow brain, till at last he was wholly bewildered.
Nearer the boat stood Alden, with one foot placed on
     the gunwale,
One still firm on the rock, and talking at times with
     the sailors,
Seated erect on the thwarts, all ready and eager for
     starting.
He too was eager to go, and thus put an end to his
     anguish,
Thinking to fly from despair, that swifter than keel is
     or canvas,

Thinking to drown in the sea the ghost that would
    rise and pursue him.
But as he gazed on the crowd, he beheld the form
    of Priscilla
Standing dejected among them, unconscious of all that
    was passing.
Fixed were her eyes upon his, as if she divined his
    intention,
Fixed with a look so sad, so reproachful, imploring,
    and patient,
That with a sudden revulsion his heart recoiled from
    its purpose,
As from the verge of a crag, where one step more
    is destruction.
Strange is the heart of man, with its quick, mysterious
    instincts!
Strange is the life of man, and fatal or fated are mo-
    ments,
Whereupon turn, as on hinges, the gates of the wall
    adamantine!
"Here I remain!" he exclaimed, as he looked at the
    heavens above him,
Thanking the Lord whose breath had scattered the mist
    and the madness,
Wherein, blind and lost, to death he was staggering
    headlong.
"Yonder snow-white cloud, that floats in the ether above
    me,
Seems like a hand that is pointing and beckoning over
    the ocean.
There is another hand, that is not so spectral and ghost-
    like,
Holding me, drawing me back, and clasping mine for
    protection.
Float, O hand of cloud, and vanish away in the ether!

Roll thyself up like a fist, to threaten and daunt me;
  I heed not
Either your warning or menace, or any omen of evil!
There is no land so sacred, no air so pure and so
  wholesome,
As is the air she breathes, and the soil that is pressed
  by her footsteps.
Here for her sake will I stay, and like an invisible
  presence
Hover around her forever, protecting, supporting her
  weakness;
Yes! as my foot was the first that stepped on this rock
  at the landing,
So, with the blessing of God, shall it be the last at
  the leaving!"

Meanwhile the Master alert, but with dignified air
  and important,
Scanning with watchful eye the tide and the wind and
  the weather,
Walked about on the sands, and the people crowded
  around him
Saying a few last words, and enforcing his careful
  remembrance.
Then, taking each by the hand, as if he were grasping
  a tiller,
Into the boat he sprang, and in haste shoved off to
  his vessel,
Glad in his heart to get rid of all this worry and
  flurry,
Glad to be gone from a land of sand and sickness and
  sorrow,
Short allowance of victual, and plenty of nothing but
  Gospel!
Lost in the sound of the oars was the last farewell of
  the Pilgrims.

O strong hearts and true! not one went back in the
    Mayflower!
No, not one looked back, who had set his hand to
    this ploughing!

Soon were heard on board the shouts and songs of
    the sailors
Heaving the windlass round, hoisting the ponderous
    anchor.
Then the yards were braced, and all sails set to the
    west wind,
Blowing steady and strong; and the *Mayflower* sailed
    from the harbor,
Rounded the point of the Gurnet, and leaving far to
    the southward
Island and cape of sand, and the Field of the First
    Encounter,
Took the wind on her quarter, and stood for the open
    Atlantic,
Borne on the send of the sea, and the swelling hearts
    of the Pilgrims.

Long in silence they watched the receding sail of the
    vessel,
Much endeared to them all, as something living and
    human;
Then, as if filled with the spirit, and wrapt in a vision
    prophetic,
Baring his hoary head, the excellent Elder of Plymouth
Said, "Let us pray!" and they prayed, and thanked the
    Lord and took courage.
Mournfully sobbed the waves at the base of the rock,
    and above them
Bowed and whispered the wheat on the hill of death,
    and their kindred

Seemed to awake in their graves, and to join in the
     prayer that they uttered.
Sun-illumined and white, on the eastern verge of the
     ocean
Gleamed the departing sail, like a marble slab in a
     graveyard;
Buried beneath it lay forever all hope of escaping.
Lo! as they turned to depart, they saw the form of
     an Indian,
Watching them from the hill; but while they spake
     with each other,
Pointing with outstretched hands, and saying, "Look!"
     he had vanished.
So they returned to their homes; but Alden lingered
     a little,
Musing alone on the shore, and watching the wash of
     the billows
Round the base of the rock, and the sparkle and flash
     of the sunshine,
Like the spirit of God, moving visibly over the waters.

VI

PRISCILLA

Thus for a while he stood, and mused by the shore
     of the ocean,
Thinking of many things, and most of all of Priscilla;
And as if thought had the power to draw to itself,
     like the loadstone,
Whatsoever it touches, by subtle laws of its nature,
Lo! as he turned to depart, Priscilla was standing beside
     him.

"Are you so much offended, you will not speak to
    me?" said she.
"Am I so much to blame, that yesterday, when you
    were pleading
Warmly the cause of another, my heart, impulsive and
    wayward,
Pleaded your own, and spake out, forgetful perhaps of
    decorum?
Certainly you can forgive me for speaking so frankly,
    for saying
What I ought not to have said, yet now I can never
    unsay it;
For there are moments in life, when the heart is so
    full of emotion,
That if by chance it be shaken, or into its depths like
    a pebble
Drops some careless word, it overflows, and its secret,
Spilt on the ground like water, can never be gathered
    together.
Yesterday I was shocked, when I heard you speak of
    Miles Standish,
Praising his virtues, transforming his very defects into
    virtues,
Praising his courage and strength, and even his fighting
    in Flanders,
As if by fighting alone you could win the heart of
    a woman,
Quite overlooking yourself and the rest, in exalting
    your hero.
Therefore I spake as I did, by an irresistible impulse.
You will forgive me, I hope, for the sake of the
    friendship between us,
Which is too true and too sacred to be so easily broken!"
Thereupon answered John Alden, the scholar, the friend
    of Miles Standish

"I was not angry with you, with myself alone I was
    angry,
Seeing how badly I managed the matter I had in my
    keeping."
"No!" interrupted the maiden, with answer prompt and
    decisive;
"No; you were angry with me, for speaking so frankly
    and freely.
It was wrong, I acknowledge; for it is the fate of a
    woman
Long to be patient and silent, to wait like a ghost that
    is speechless,
Till some questioning voice dissolves the spell of its
    silence.
Hence in the inner life of so many suffering women
Sunless and silent and deep, like subterranean rivers
Running through caverns of darkness, unheard, unseen,
    and unfruitful,
Chafing their channels of stone, with endless and profitless
    murmurs."
Thereupon answered John Alden, the young man, the
    lover of women:
"Heaven forbid it, Priscilla; and truly they seem to me
    always
More like the beautiful rivers that watered the Garden
    of Eden,
More like the river Euphrates, through deserts of Havilah
    flowing,
Filling the land with delight, and memories sweet of
    the garden!"
"Ah, by these words, I can see," again interrupted the
    maiden,
"How very little you prize me, or care for what I am
    saying.
When from the depths of my heart, in pain and with
    secret misgiving,

Frankly I speak to you, asking for sympathy only and
    kindness,
Straightway you take up my words, that are plain and
    direct and in earnest,
Turn them away from their meaning, and answer with
    flattering phrases.
This is not right, is not just, is not true to the best
    that is in you;
For I know and esteem you, and feel that your nature
    is noble,
Lifting mine up to a higher, a more ethereal level.
Therefore I value your friendship, and feel it perhaps
    the more keenly
If you say aught that implies I am only as one among
    many,
If you make use of those common and complimentary
    phrases
Most men think so fine, in dealing and speaking with
    women,
But which women reject as insipid, if not as insulting."

Mute and amazed was Alden; and listened and looked
    at Priscilla,
Thinking he never had seen her more fair, more divine
    in her beauty.
He who but yesterday pleaded so glibly the cause of
    another,
Stood there embarrassed and silent, and seeking in vain
    for an answer.
So the maiden went on, and little divined or imagined
What was at work in his heart, that made him so
    awkward and speechless.
"Let us then, be what we are, and speak what we
    think, and in all things
Keep ourselves loyal to truth, and the sacred professions
    of friendship.

It is no secret I tell you, nor am I ashamed to declare
    it:
I have liked to be with you, to see you, to speak
    with you always.
So I was hurt at your words, and a little affronted
    to hear you
Urge me to marry your friend, though he were the
    Captain Miles Standish.
For I must tell you the truth: much more to me is
    your friendship
Than all the love he could give, were he twice the
    hero you think him."
Then she extended her hand, and Alden, who eagerly
    grasped it,
Felt all the wounds in his heart, that were aching and
    bleeding so sorely,
Healed by the touch of that hand, and he said, with
    a voice full of feeling:
"Yes, we must ever be friends; and of all who offer
    you friendship
Let me be ever the first, the truest, the nearest and
    dearest!"

Casting a farewell look at the glimmering sail of the
    Mayflower,
Distant, but still in sight, and sinking below the horizon,
Homeward together they walked, with a strange, indefi-
    nite feeling,
That all the rest had departed and left them alone in
    the desert.
But, as they went through the fields in the blessing
    and smile of the sunshine,
Lighter grew their hearts, and Priscilla said very archly:
"Now that our terrible Captain has gone in pursuit of
    the Indians,

Where he is happier far than he would be commanding
    a household,
You may speak boldly, and tell me of all that happened
    between you,
When you returned last night, and said how ungrateful
    you found me."
Thereupon answered John Alden, and told her the whole
    of the story,—
Told her his own despair, and the direful wrath of
    Miles Standish.
Whereat the maiden smiled, and said between laughing
    and earnest,
"He is a little chimney, and heated hot in a moment!"
But as he gently rebuked her, and told her how he
    had suffered,—
How he had even determined to sail that day in the
    Mayflower,
And had remained for her sake, on hearing the dangers
    that threatened,—
All her manner was changed, and she said with a
    faltering accent,
"Truly I thank you for this: how good you have been
    to me always!"

Thus, as a pilgrim devout, who toward Jerusalem
    journeys,
Taking three steps in advance, and one reluctantly
    backward,
Urged by importunate zeal, and withheld by pangs of
    contrition;
Slowly but steadily onward, receding yet ever advancing,
Journeyed this Puritan youth to the Holy Land of his
    longings,
Urged by the fervor of love, and withheld by remorseful
    misgivings.

VII

THE MARCH OF MILES STANDISH

Meanwhile the stalwart Miles Standish was marching
    steadily northward,
Winding through forest and swamp, and along the trend
    of the seashore,
All day long, with hardly a halt, the fire of his anger
Burning and crackling within, and the sulphurous odor
    of powder
Seeming more sweet to his nostrils than all the scents
    of the forest.
Silent and moody he went, and much he revolved his
    discomfort;
He who was used to success, and to easy victories
    always,
Thus to be flouted, rejected, and laughed to scorn by
    a maiden,
Thus to be mocked and betrayed by the friend whom
    most he had trusted!
Ah! 't was too much to be borne, and he fretted and
    chafed in his armor!

"I alone am to blame," he muttered, "for mine was
    the folly.
What has a rough old soldier, grown grim and gray
    in the harness,
Used to the camp and its ways, to do with the wooing
    of maidens?
'T was but a dream,—let it pass,—let it vanish like
    so many others!
What I thought was a flower, is only a weed, and is
    worthless;
Out of my heart will I pluck it, and throw it away,
    and henceforward

Be but a fighter of battles, a lover and wooer of
    dangers!"
Thus he revolved in his mind his sorry defeat and
    discomfort,
While he was marching by day or lying at night in
    the forest,
Looking up at the trees, and the constellations beyond
    them.

After a three days' march he came to an Indian
    encampment
Pitched on the edge of a meadow, between the sea
    and the forest;
Women at work by the tents, and warriors, horrid
    with war paint,
Seated about a fire, and smoking and talking together;
Who, when they saw from afar the sudden approach
    of the white men,
Saw the flash of the sun on breastplate and sabre and
    musket,
Straightway leaped to their feet, and two, from among
    them advancing,
Came to parley with Standish, and offer him furs as
    a present;
Friendship was in their looks, but in their hearts there
    was hatred.
Braves of the tribe were these, and brothers, gigantic
    in stature,
Huge as Goliath of Gath, or the terrible Og, king of
    Bashan;
One was Pecksuot named, and the other was called
    Wattawamat.
Round their necks were suspended their knives in
    scabbards of wampum,
Two-edged, trenchant knives, with points as sharp as
    a needle.

Other arms had they none, for they were cunning and
    crafty.
"Welcome, English!" they said,—these words they had
    learned from the traders
Touching at times on the coast, to barter and chaffer
    for peltries.
Then in their native tongue they began to parley with
    Standish,
Through his guide and interpreter, Hobomok, friend
    of the white man,
Begging for blankets and knives, but mostly for muskets
    and powder,
Kept by the white man, they said, concealed, with the
    plague, in his cellars,
Ready to be let loose, and destroy his brother the red
    man!
But when Standish refused, and said he would give
    them the Bible,
Suddenly changing their tone, they began to boast and
    to bluster.
Then Wattawamat advanced with a stride in front of
    the other,
And, with a lofty demeanor, thus vauntingly spake to
    the Captain:
"Now Wattawamat can see, by the fiery eyes of the
    Captain,
Angry is he in his heart; but the heart of the brave
    Wattawamat
Is not afraid at the sight. He was not born of a woman,
But on a mountain at night, from an oak tree riven
    by lightning,
Forth he sprang at a bound, with all his weapons about
    him,
Shouting, 'Who is there here to fight with the brave
    Wattawamat?' "

Then he unsheathed his knife, and, whetting the blade
  on his left hand,
Held it aloft and displayed a woman's face on the
  handle;
Saying, with bitter expression and look of sinister
  meaning:
"I have another at home, with the face of a man on
  the handle;
By and by they shall marry; and there will be plenty
  of children!"

Then stood Pecksuot forth, self-vaunting, insulting
  Miles Standish:
While with his fingers he patted the knife that hung
  at his bosom,
Drawing it half from its sheath, and plunging it back,
  as he muttered,
"By and by it shall see; it shall eat; ah, ha! but shall
  speak not!
This is the mighty Captain the white men have sent
  to destroy us!
He is a little man; let him go and work with the
  women!"

Meanwhile Standish had noted the faces and figures
  of Indians
Peeping and creeping about from bush to tree in the
  forest,
Feigning to look for game, with arrows set on their
  bow strings,
Drawing about him still closer and closer the net of
  their ambush.
But undaunted he stood, and dissembled and treated
  them smoothly;
So the old chronicles say, that were writ in the days
  of the fathers.

But when he heard their defiance, the boast, the taunt,
and the insult,
All the hot blood of his race, of Sir Hugh and of
Thurston de Standish,
Boiled and beat in his heart, and swelled in the veins
of his temples.
Headlong he leaped on the boaster, and, snatching his
knife from its scabbard,
Plunged it into his heart, and, reeling backward, the
savage
Fell with his face to the sky, and a fiendlike fierceness
upon it.
Straight there arose from the forest the awful sound
of the war whoop,
And, like a flurry of snow on the whistling wind of
December,
Swift and sudden and keen came a flight of feathery
arrows.
Then came a cloud of smoke, and out of the cloud
came the lightning,
Out of the lightning thunder; and death unseen ran
before it.
Frightened the savages fled for shelter in swamp and
in thicket,
Hotly pursued and beset; but their sachem, the brave
Wattawamat,
Fled not; he was dead. Unswerving and swift had a
bullet
Passed through his brain, and he fell with both hands
clutching the greensward,
Seeming in death to hold back from his foe the land
of his fathers.

There on the flowers of the meadow the warriors
lay, and above them,

Silent, with folded arms, stood Hobomok, friend of the white man.

Smiling at length he exclaimed to the stalwart Captain of Plymouth:

"Pecksuot bragged very loud, of his courage, his strength, and his stature,—

Mocked the great Captain, and called him a little man; but I see now

Big enough have you been to lay him speechless before you!"

Thus the first battle was fought and won by the stalwart Miles Standish.

When the tidings thereof were brought to the village of Plymouth,

And as a trophy of war the head of the brave Wattawamat

Scowled from the roof of the fort, which at once was a church and a fortress,

All who beheld it rejoiced, and praised the Lord, and took courage.

Only Priscilla averted her face from this specter of terror,

Thanking God in her heart that she had not married Miles Standish;

Shrinking, fearing almost, lest, coming home from his battles,

He should lay claim to her hand, as the prize and reward of his valor.

VIII

THE SPINNING WHEEL

Month after month passed away, and in autumn the
  ships of the merchants
Came with kindred and friends, with cattle and corn
  for the Pilgrims.
All in the village was peace; the men were intent on
  their labors,
Busy with hewing and building, with garden plot and
  with merestead,
Busy with breaking the glebe, and mowing the grass
  in the meadows,
Searching the sea for its fish, and hunting the deer in
  the forest.
All in the village was peace; but at times the rumor
  of warfare
Filled the air with alarm, and the apprehension of danger.
Bravely the stalwart Standish was scouring the land
  with his forces,
Waxing valiant in fight and defeating the alien armies,
Till his name had become a sound of fear to the
  nations.
Anger was still in his heart, but at times the remorse
  and contrition
Which in all noble natures succeed the passionate out-
  break,
Came like a rising tide, that encounters the rush of
  a river,
Staying its current awhile, but making it bitter and
  brackish.

Meanwhile Alden at home had built him a new
  habitation,
Solid, substantial, of timber rough-hewn from the firs
  of the forest.

Wooden-barred was the door, and the roof was covered
with rushes;
Latticed the windows were, and the windowpanes were
of paper,
Oiled to admit the light, while wind and rain were
excluded.
There too he dug a well, and around it planted an
orchard:
Still may be seen to this day some trace of the well
and the orchard.
Close to the house was the stall, where, safe and secure
from annoyance,
Raghorn, the snow-white bull, that had fallen to Alden's
allotment
In the division of cattle, might ruminate in the nighttime;
Over the pastures he cropped, made fragrant by sweet
pennyroyal.

Oft when his labor was finished, with eager feet
would the dreamer
Follow the pathway that ran through the woods to the
house of Priscilla,
Led by illusions romantic and subtle deceptions of
fancy,
Pleasure disguised as duty, and love in the semblance
of friendship.
Ever of her he thought, when he fashioned the walls
of his dwelling;
Ever of her he thought, when he delved in the soil
of his garden;
Ever of her he thought when he read in his Bible on
Sunday
Praise of the virtuous woman, as she is described in
the Proverbs,—
How the heart of her husband doth safely trust in her
always,

How all the days of her life she will do him good,
    and not evil,
How she seeketh the wool and the flax and worketh
    with gladness,
How she layeth her hand to the spindle and holdeth
    the distaff,
How she is not afraid of the snow for herself or her
    household,
Knowing her household are clothed with the scarlet
    cloth of her weaving!

So as she sat at her wheel one afternoon in the
    autumn,
Alden, who opposite sat, and was watching her dexterous
    fingers,
As if the thread she was spinning were that of his life
    and his fortune,
After a pause in their talk, thus spake to the sound
    of the spindle.
"Truly, Priscilla," he said, "when I see you spinning
    and spinning,
Never idle a moment, but thrifty and thoughtful of
    others,
Suddenly you are transformed, are visibly changed in
    a moment;
You are no longer Priscilla, but Bertha the Beautiful
    Spinner."
Here the light foot on the treadle grew swifter and
    swifter; the spindle
Uttered an angry snarl, and the thread snapped short
    in her fingers;
While the impetuous speaker, not heeding the mischief,
    continued:
"You are the beautiful Bertha, the spinner, the queen
    of Helvetia;
She whose story I read at a stall in the streets of
    Southampton,

Who, as she rode on her palfrey, o'er valley and meadow
and mountain,
Ever was spinning her thread from a distaff fixed to
her saddle.
She was so thrifty and good, that her name passed
into a proverb.
So shall it be with your own, when the spinning wheel
shall no longer
Hum in the house of the farmer, and fill its chambers
with music.
Then shall the mothers, reproving, relate how it was
in their childhood,
Praising the good old times, and the days of Priscilla
the spinner!"
Straight uprose from her wheel the beautiful Puritan
maiden,
Pleased with the praise of her thrift from him whose
praise was the sweetest,
Drew from the reel on the table a snowy skein of her
spinning,
Thus making answer, meanwhile, to the flattering phrases
of Alden:
"Come, you must not be idle; if I am a pattern for
housewives,
Show yourself equally worthy of being the model of
husbands.
Hold this skein on your hands, while I wind it, ready
for knitting;
Then who knows but hereafter, when fashions have
changed and the manners,
Fathers may talk to their sons of the good old times
of John Alden!"
Thus, with a jest and a laugh, the skein on his hands
she adjusted,
He sitting awkwardly there, with his arms extended
before him,

She standing graceful, erect, and winding the thread
     from his fingers,
Sometimes chiding a little his clumsy manner of holding,
Sometimes touching his hands, as she disentangled ex-
     pertly
Twist or knot in the yarn, unawares—for how could
     she help it?—
Sending electrical thrills through every nerve in his body.

Lo! in the midst of this scene, a breathless messenger
     entered,
Bringing in hurry and heat the terrible news from the
     village.
Yes; Miles Standish was dead!—an Indian had brought
     them the tidings,—
Slain by a poisoned arrow, shot down in the front of
     the battle,
Into an ambush beguiled, cut off with the whole of
     his forces;
All the town would be burned, and all the people be
     murdered!
Such were the tidings of evil that burst on the hearts
     of the hearers.
Silent and statuelike stood Priscilla, her face looking
     backward
Still at the face of the speaker, her arms uplifted in
     horror;
But John Alden, upstarting, as if the barb of the arrow
Piercing the heart of his friend had struck his own,
     and had sundered
Once and forever the bonds that held him bound as
     a captive,
Wild with excess of sensation, the awful delight of his
     freedom,
Mingled with pain and regret, unconscious of what he
     was doing,

Clasped, almost with a groan, the motionless form of
    Priscilla,
Pressing her close to his heart, as forever his own,
    and exclaiming:
"Those whom the Lord hath united, let no man put
    them asunder!"

Even as rivulets twain, from distant and separate
    sources,
Seeing each other afar, as they leap from the rocks,
    and pursuing
Each one its devious path, but drawing nearer and
    nearer,
Rush together at last, at their trysting-place in the forest;
So these lives that had run thus far in separate channels,
Coming in sight of each other, then swerving and
    flowing asunder,
Parted by barriers strong, but drawing nearer and nearer,
Rushed together at last, and one was lost in the other.

IX

THE WEDDING DAY

Forth from the curtain of clouds, from the tent of
    purple and scarlet,
Issued the sun, the great High Priest, in his garments
    resplendent,
Holiness unto the Lord, in letters of light, on his
    forehead,
Round the hem of his robe the golden bells and
    pomegranates.
Blessing the world he came, and the bars of vapor
    beneath him
Gleamed like a grate of brass, and the sea at his feet
    was a laver!

This was the wedding morn of Priscilla the Puritan
maiden.
Friends were assembled together; the Elder and Mag-
istrate also
Graced the scene with their presence, and stood like
the Law and the Gospel,
One with the sanction of earth and one with the blessing
of heaven.
Simple and brief was the wedding, as that of Ruth
and of Boaz.
Softly the youth and the maiden repeated the words
of betrothal,
Taking each other for husband and wife in the Magistrate's
presence,
After the Puritan way, and the laudable custom of
Holland.
Fervently then, and devoutly, the excellent Elder of
Plymouth
Prayed for the hearth and the home, that were founded
that day in affection,
Speaking of life and of death, and imploring Divine
benedictions.

Lo! When the service was ended, a form appeared
on the threshold,
Clad in armor of steel, a somber and sorrowful figure!
Why does the bridegroom start and stare at the strange
apparition?
Why does the bride turn pale, and hide her face on
his shoulder?
Is it a phantom of air,—a bodiless, spectral illusion?
Is it a ghost from the grave, that has come to forbid
the betrothal?
Long had it stood there unseen, a guest uninvited,
unwelcomed;

Over its clouded eyes there had passed at times an
expression
Softening the gloom and revealing the warm heart hidden
beneath them,
As when across the sky the driving rack of the raincloud
Grows for a moment thin, and betrays the sun by its
brightness.
Once it had lifted its hand, and moved its lips, but
was silent,
As if an iron will had mastered the fleeting intention.
But when were ended the troth and the prayer and
the last benediction,
Into the room it strode, and the people beheld with
amazement
Bodily there in his armor Miles Standish, the Captain
of Plymouth!
Grasping the bridegroom's hand, he said with emotion,
"Forgive me!
I have been angry and hurt,—too long have I cherished
the feeling;
I have been cruel and hard, but now, thank God! it
is ended.
Mine is the same hot blood that leaped in the veins
of Hugh Standish,
Sensitive, swift to resent, but as swift in atoning for
error.
Never so much as now was Miles Standish the friend
of John Alden."
Thereupon answered the bridegroom: "Let all be for-
gotten between us,—
All save the dear, old friendship, and that shall grow
older and dearer!"
Then the Captain advanced, and, bowing, saluted Pris-
cilla,
Gravely, and after the manner of old-fashioned gentry
in England,

Something of camp and of court, of town and of
  country, commingled,
Wishing her joy of her wedding, and loudly lauding
  her husband.
Then he said with a smile: "I should have remembered
  the adage,
If you would be well served, you must serve yourself;
  and moreover,
No man can gather cherries in Kent at the season of
  Christmas!"

Great was the people's amazement, and greater yet
  their rejoicing,
Thus to behold once more the sunburnt face of their
  Captain,
Whom they had mourned as dead; and they gathered
  and crowded about him,
Eager to see him and hear him, forgetful of bride and
  of bridegroom,
Questioning, answering, laughing, and each interrupting
  the other,
Till the good Captain declared, being quite overpowered
  and bewildered,
He had rather by far break into an Indian encampment,
Than come again to a wedding to which he had not
  been invited.

Meanwhile the bridegroom went forth and stood with
  the bride at the doorway,
Breathing the perfumed air of that warm and beautiful
  morning.
Touched with autumnal tints, but lonely and sad in
  the sunshine,
Lay extended before them the land of toil and privation;
There were the graves of the dead, and the barren
  waste of the seashore,

There the familiar fields, the groves of pine, and the
  meadows;
But to their eyes transfigured, it seemed as the Garden
  of Eden,
Filled with the presence of God, whose voice was the
  sound of the ocean.

Soon was their vision disturbed by the noise and stir
  of departure,
Friends coming forth from the house, and impatient of
  longer delaying,
Each with his plan for the day, and the work that
  was left uncompleted,
Then, from a stall near at hand, amid exclamations of
  wonder,
Alden the thoughtful, the careful, so happy, so proud
  of Priscilla,
Brought out his snow-white bull, obeying the hand of
  its master,
Led by a cord that was tied to an iron ring in its
  nostrils,
Covered with crimson cloth, and a cushion placed for
  a saddle.
She should not walk, he said, through the dust and
  heat of the noonday;
Nay, she should ride like a queen, not plod along like
  a peasant.
Somewhat alarmed at first, but reassured by the others,
Placing her hand on the cushion, her foot in the hand
  of her husband,
Gayly, with joyous laugh, Priscilla mounted her palfrey.
"Nothing is wanting now," he said with a smile, "but
  the distaff;
Then you would be in truth my queen, my beautiful
  Bertha!"

Onward the bridal procession now moved to their
    new habitation,
Happy husband and wife, and friends conversing together.
Pleasantly murmured the brook, as they crossed the
    ford in the forest,
Pleased with the image that passed, like a dream of
    love through its bosom,
Tremulous, floating in air, o'er the depths of the azure
    abysses.
Down through the golden leaves the sun was pouring
    his splendors,
Gleaming on purple grapes, that, from branches above
    them suspended,
Mingled their odorous breath with the balm of the pine
    and the fir tree,
Wild and sweet as the clusters that grew in the valley
    of Eschol.
Like a picture it seemed of the primitive, pastoral ages,
Fresh with the youth of the world, and recalling Rebecca
    and Isaac,
Old and yet ever new, and simple and beautiful always,
Love immortal and young in the endless succession of
    lovers.
So through the Plymouth woods passed onward the
    bridal procession.